MINUTEMEALS

5-INGREDIENT MAIN DISHES
Creative, Streamlined Menus in 20 Minutes

Edited by Miriam Garron

BARNES
& NOBLE

NEW YORK

2006 Barnes & Noble Books

ISBN 0-7607-7781-0

Printed and bound in China

06 07 08 09 10 11 M 9 8 7 6 5 4 3 2 1

welcome to *5-ingredient main dishes,*

the fourth cookbook in the minutemeals series. Many of you are old hands with the minutemeals method, either as visitors to our website, minutemeals.com, or as collectors of our previous cookbooks. If this is your first minutemeals book, get ready to join the satisfied people who have rediscovered the pleasure of home cooking and the family dinner.

pleasure? In the midst of most families' hectic schedules, obligation might more accurately describe your dinner preparation. Or maybe you avoid preparation altogether, and, three out of five weeknights, your family members eat a meal that comes from a can, a box, or a takeout bag.

minutemeals can change that. The minutemeals method helps you plan, shop, cook, and serve meals that will bring the family to the table to eat, to talk, and to reconnect. Every minutemeals menu is carefully crafted so that a complete dinner can be on the table in 20 minutes. Each of the 80 menus in this book includes shopping and pantry lists, an "at-a-glance" gameplan of the steps in the menu, and useful tips from the professional chefs who developed the menus. And to make sure your minutemeals experience starts the minute you open the book, we designed the pages to be as clean and efficient as the menus themselves.

this book takes minutemeals efficiency and creativity one step further: Every dish—not just the main dish but every side, salad, and dessert— contains no more than five easy-to-find ingredients. No big deal, of course, if you simply open a box and add water to make a meal. But when we promise home-cooked meals, we mean cooked: Our chefs combine fresh, contemporary ingredients with prepared—but not overly processed—foods to produce the kinds of dishes that we remember from the family meals of our childhood.

with 80 menus to choose from, you'll soon build a repertoire of easy, fast recipes done the minutemeals way. So if you're new here, you'll soon be serving your family the kinds of meals you've dreamed of serving but didn't think you could. If you're back, you'll be delighted that we've done it again, creating keepsake five-ingredient, 20-minute meals—meals you can really count on.

Miriam Garron, *Editor*

minutemeals
5-ingredient main dishes

meet the minutemeals chefs

We'd like you to meet the chefs behind minutemeals, the people whose creativity and ingenuity created the delicious menus in this book. Their combined expertise is our ace in the hole—the secret that keeps our menus fresh, interesting, and full of great ideas. You'll find their helpful comments throughout the book, paired with the menus they created.

Nancy Allen

David Bonom

Lisa Cherkasky

Hillary Davis-Tonken

Ruth Fisher

Miriam Garron

Wendy Kalen

Paul E. Piccuito

Sarah Reynolds

Patty Santelli

how to use this book

minutemeals 5-ingredient main dishes is designed to be as efficient as possible. Twenty minutes, after all, is a short amount of time to cook a full meal and place it on the table. For you to be able to do the cooking with as few setbacks as possible, we took care of as many of the time-consuming details as we could. Rely on our system and you will have a delicious dinner on the table in 20 minutes.

Each menu includes a shopping list of the major ingredients needed, as well as a complete list of ingredients we consider standard pantry items. No more hunting through multiple recipes to glean what you need to buy on the way home— we've done that for you. Our "menu **gameplan**" then orders the sequence of just how to go about cooking the meal—what dish needs to be started first, what

should follow, and so on. We've also noted when to preheat the oven or broiler so that it will be sufficiently heated for maximum cooking results, and when you need to put water on to boil for pasta and rice. The double-page format of each menu guarantees that when you refer to the cooking directions of any given dish you are always on the "same page."

The recipes here help you make great-tasting meals using just 5 ingredients. And because we know you don't want to spend more time shopping than cooking, we chose easy-to-find, family-friendly ingredients, including prepared foods. In recipes that call for water, cooking spray, salt, or pepper, we've listed those ingredients— staples in even the most sparsely stocked kitchen—in the recipe instructions. We recommend that you read through the menu before you start cooking so that you can have everything you need on the counter before you begin.

The minutemeals clock starts ticking when you put the ingredients for a menu on the kitchen counter. The first several times you make a menu, expect it to take a few minutes more than you had anticipated: The system itself and the recipes are new to you, and, as the saying goes, practice makes perfect. Once you've had the practice, we know that you will find the results delicious . . . and quick.

quick tips from the pros

tanya holland

doctorin' it up

that's a soul-kitchen term for adding just a pinch of something to a plain-tasting dish in order to "bring the taste home." The pinch doesn't have to be from the soul pantry; spice blends and herbs from 'round the world can really add flavor on the fly—that is, *now!*

old bay seasoning: This quintessential seafood spice just sits on folks' shelves between once-a-year-crab boils. It shouldn't! I add it to everything from crab cakes to shrimp cocktail to tuna salad.

garam masala: Recipes for this Indian spice blend vary, but the blend generally includes warm, fragrant spices such as cumin, cloves, black pepper, nutmeg, cardamom, and cinnamon. Now, who has time to measure out every one of those? I add this spice blend to everything from stir-fries to carrot muffin mix in order to add an exotic, ethnic flavor.

herbes de provence: Not a spice but a dried herb blend of rosemary, thyme, and perhaps savory, marjoram, or lavender, it's a sure-fire way to bring the taste of the Côte d'Azur to everything from sautéed vegetables to roast chicken.

fresh herbs: Buy at least one fresh green herb even when you're relying on prepared foods for dinner. Whenever I buy prepared potato salad, for example, I add fresh parsley, cilantro, dill, or chives. Snip the herbs and stir in just before serving to get maximum flavor and color.

Tanya Holland, a chef/host of the Food Network's *Melting Pot* program, takes a multi-ethnic approach to her cooking, combining Caribbean, Mediterranean, and Southern influences with classic French technique. After earning a B.A. in Russian language and literature from the University of Virginia and a culinary degree from France's La Varenne cooking school, Tanya cooked around the world, working with chefs in New York City, Boston, and France. Tanya also works as a food stylist and teacher and has contributed articles to *Food and Wine* and *Signature Bride* magazines.

lidia matticchio bastianich

coaxing the most from simple ingredients

fresh-frozen herbs give you the flavor of fresh and the convenience of dried. Not all supermarkets carry a consistently good selection of fresh herbs, so when you find some, use this trick to preserve them as close to their fresh state as possible: Place the leaves in small paper or plastic cups, fill with water, and freeze. When frozen, pop the cubes out of the cups and pack them in self-sealing bags. The herbs stay fresh and green this way for months—I defrost the cubes or just plop them into sauces and stews as I need them.

when i'm making a sauce, a stew, or pasta, i add half the butter or olive oil at the beginning of the cooking process and the remaining half at the end. A tablespoon of butter or olive oil stirred into a finished dish or tossed with pasta adds depth and body to the finished dish because the flavor doesn't "cook out."

if a sauce is too thin, stirring in dried bread crumbs is an efficient way to thicken it. All-purpose flour added to a sauce at the last minute can impart an unpleasant, raw flour flavor that takes a few minutes to cook out. I substitute dried bread crumbs in shellfish braises or meat stews to achieve a thick, velvety sauce in 5 minutes or so, then strain the sauce before serving.

Star of the series *Lidia's Italian American Kitchen* and *Lidia's Italian Table,* Lidia Bastianich is also the author of the companion books to each series, as well as *La Cucina di Lidia* and *Lidia's Italian Table,* a syndicated column distributed by Universal Press. Lidia owns the award-winning Felidia and Becco restaurants and is a partner with her son Joseph and Mario Batali in Esca, all in New York City. She also co-owns eponymous restaurants in Kansas City, Missouri, and in Pittsburgh. In 1998, Lidia launched her own line of pasta sauces, and she now also produces an exclusive line for Williams-Sonoma.

corinna mozo

less is more

less is truly more when you cook "en papillote"— that is, in tightly sealed parchment or foil packets. You don't want a lot of competing flavors, just a few clean ones. The packets trap all of the juices, making the finished dish moist and flavorful. I cook skinless boneless chicken breasts this way, but you can use fish fillets or shrimp—any quick-cooking ingredient. Add a mix of colorful vegetables from the salad bar such as sliced zucchini, carrots, or peppers, or a couple of snow peas. Finally, raid the pantry for capers, garlic, lemon zest, a pat of butter, a sprinkle of fresh or dried herbs, or a splash of olive oil or wine, and seal tightly. Most people roast the packages, but I throw them in a hot, lightly oiled skillet for 7 to 8 minutes—that way I don't heat up the kitchen. And the packages can be assembled and sealed in advance—what could be easier?

grill the best fish ever with just some water and salt. Smearing a whole fish and the grill rack with oil can cause flare-ups that char the delicate flesh of the fish. So I brush the fish and the hot grill rack with a solution of 2 parts salt to 1 part water. The water keeps the fish from sticking to the grill and produces evenly cooked, moist fish.

use a coffee grinder to grind fresh spices as you need them. Freshly ground spices pack so much flavor that just a sprinkle adds intense flavor to any main ingredient. I grind cumin and cardamom for chicken, star anise and cloves for pork, and juniper berries for venison.

Corinna Mozo is the founder and executive chef of Boston's renowned Truc. In 1998, *The Wine Spectator* listed her as a "Rising Star of American Cuisine"; in 1996, Julia Child and The American Institute of Food and Wine honored her as one of the best chefs in Boston. Corinna has appeared on various Food Network programs and on the Discovery Channel's *Home Matters.*

minute
5-ingredient

main-course soup and salad menus

meals

main dishes

florentine tortellini soup

with spinach and basil

tossed salad with marinated tomatoes

seeded breadsticks

cassata in a cup

menugameplan

serves 4

step	1	assemble the **tossed salad with marinated tomatoes**
step	2	cook the **florentine tortellini soup with spinach and basil**
step	3	assemble the **cassata in a cup**
step	4	**serve**

shopping list

Grape tomatoes

Balsamic vinaigrette salad dressing, store-bought or homemade

Prewashed Italian salad mix

Zucchini

Fresh refrigerated cheese tortellini

Prewashed baby spinach

Refrigerated basil pesto

Pound cake

Ricotta cheese

Miniature chocolate chips

Raspberries

Seeded breadsticks

from your pantry

Salt

Freshly ground black pepper

Fat-free reduced-sodium chicken broth

Orange juice

Confectioners' sugar

headsup

Whether you call them tortellini or capelletti, these stuffed pastas are increasingly available in supermarket refrigerator sections, with fillings ranging from simple cheese or meat to more intriguing exotic mushroom or pumpkin. We use cheese-filled here, but feel free to experiment, or substitute mini ravioli if you can't find the tortellini.

"This soup takes so little effort, I can add it to a dinner-party menu without any complication."

—minutemeals' chef Sarah

step 1

assemble the **tossed salad with marinated tomatoes**

1 container (1 pint)
grape tomatoes

3 tablespoons balsamic
vinaigrette salad dressing

1 bag (10 ounces) prewashed
Italian salad mix

Combine the grape tomatoes, salt and pepper to taste, and salad dressing in a salad bowl. Add the greens and place the bowl on the table; do not toss until serving time.

step 2

cook the **florentine tortellini soup with spinach and basil**

1 can (48 ounces) fat-free
reduced-sodium chicken broth

1 medium zucchini, diced

1 1/2 packages (9 ounces each)
fresh cheese tortellini

1 bag (6 ounces) baby spinach

1/3 cup refrigerated basil pesto

1. Put the broth in a large pot or Dutch oven. Cover the pot and bring the broth to a boil over high heat. Dice the zucchini.

2. Add the tortellini to the broth and return to a boil, stirring. Cover, reduce the heat, and simmer 5 minutes. Stir in the zucchini, cover, and simmer until the tortellini are cooked through, 2 to 4 minutes longer.

3. Stir in the spinach; remove from the heat and stir in the pesto. Cover to keep hot.

step 3

assemble the **cassata in a cup**

4 slices pound cake,
cut into cubes

3 tablespoons orange juice

1/2 cup part-skim
ricotta cheese

2 tablespoons
confectioners' sugar

2 tablespoons miniature
chocolate chips

1. Cut the pound cake into cubes and divide among 4 cups or dessert dishes. Drizzle with the orange juice.

2. Place the ricotta cheese in a small bowl. Stir in the confectioners' sugar and the chocolate chips. Spoon the ricotta mixture over the pound cake.

step 4

serve

1. Ladle the soup into 4 bowls. Toss the salad; serve the breadsticks with the soup and the salad.

2. When ready for dessert, serve the cassata.

**Florentine Tortellini Soup
with Spinach and Basil**
Single serving is 1/4 of total recipe
CALORIES 266; PROTEIN 12g; CARBS 25g;
TOTAL FAT 13g; SAT FAT 3g; CHOLESTEROL 15mg;
SODIUM 1317mg; FIBER 4g

mexican bean soup
cucumber and avocado salad
cumin toasted corn muffins
tropical fruit sundaes

menu
gameplan

serves 4

beforeyoustart

Preheat the oven to 400°F to toast the muffins.

step	1	cook the **mexican bean soup**
step	2	make the **cucumber and avocado salad**
step	3	bake the **cumin toasted corn muffins**
step	4	assemble the **tropical fruit sundaes**
step	5	**serve**

shopping list

Mild salsa

Mild chili seasoning mix

Pinto beans

Frozen corn

Shredded Monterey Jack and Cheddar cheese blend

Cucumber slices
(from the salad bar)

Red onion slices
(from the salad bar)

Ripe avocado

Cilantro

Italian salad dressing

Corn muffin tops
or corn muffins

Cut-up tropical fruits
(from the produce department
or salad bar)

Fruit sorbet

from your pantry

Salt and pepper

Butter

Ground cumin

Hot paprika

Orange juice

Sugar

headsup This bean soup makes a hearty meatless meal, with the protein coming from both beans and cheese. But if there is a die-hard meat eater in your crowd, you can replace one of the cans of beans with 8 ounces of lean ground beef or turkey. Brown it first in a nonstick skillet, transfer it to a pot, and proceed with step 1.

"This menu is so simple, but there's nothing plain about it. Each recipe has real zing."

—minutemeals' chef Sarah

step 1

cook the **mexican bean soup**

1 cup mild salsa

1 package (about 1³/₈ ounces) mild chili seasoning mix

2 cans (15 to 16 ounces each) pinto beans

1 box (10 ounces) frozen corn kernels

¹/₂ cup shredded Monterey Jack and Cheddar cheese blend

1. In a large pot, stir together the salsa, chili seasoning mix, and 2 cups water. Cover and bring to a boil over high heat.

2. Meanwhile, rinse and drain the beans. Stir them into the soup along with the corn. Cover and return to a boil; reduce the heat and simmer, stirring occasionally, for 10 minutes.

step 2

make the **cucumber and avocado salad**

1¹/₂ cups cucumber slices

¹/₄ cup red onion slices

1 ripe avocado

¹/₄ cup cilantro leaves

3 tablespoons Italian salad dressing

1. Stack the cucumber slices on a cutting board and slice into thin strips. Chop the red onion. Halve, pit, and peel the avocado; cut it into cubes. Coarsely chop the cilantro.

2. Put everything in a salad bowl. Add the dressing, season with the salt and pepper to taste, and toss gently. Place the bowl on the table with 4 salad plates.

step 3

bake the **cumin toasted corn muffins**

4 corn muffin tops

1¹/₂ tablespoons butter

¹/₈ teaspoon ground cumin

¹/₈ teaspoon paprika

Preheat the oven to 400°F. Place the muffin tops on a baking sheet. (If using corn muffins, split them horizontally and, if the tops are very peaked, remove a thin slice so they will lie flat when arranged cut side up.) Cut the butter into 4 pats. Top each muffin top or half with a pat of butter. Dust each with a bit of the cumin and paprika. Bake 5 minutes, or until hot and lightly toasted.

step 4

assemble the **tropical fruit sundaes**

1¹/₂ cups cut-up fresh tropical fruit

2 tablespoons orange juice

1 tablespoon sugar

1 pint fruit sorbet, such as mango, lemon, or raspberry

Combine the fruit, orange juice, and sugar in a bowl. Scoop the sorbet into 4 dessert dishes and place in the freezer.

step 5

serve

1. Transfer the toasted muffins to a bread basket.

2. Ladle the soup into 4 bowls and sprinkle with the cheese.

3. When ready for dessert, spoon the fruit mixture over the sorbet and serve.

Mexican Bean Soup
Single serving is ¹/₄ of total recipe

CALORIES 296; PROTEIN 14g; CARBS 47g; TOTAL FAT 7g; SAT FAT 3g; CHOLESTEROL 15mg; SODIUM 1388mg; FIBER 8g

chicken gumbo soup
jarlsberg cheese and walnut salad
crusty sourdough rolls
sponge cakes with lemon curd and strawberries

menu gameplan

shopping list

Skinless boneless chicken thighs

Basil-, garlic-, and oregano-flavored diced tomatoes

Frozen mixed soup vegetables or succotash

Boil-in-the-bag red beans and rice mix

Chopped walnuts

Prewashed European salad mix

Jarlsberg cheese

Balsamic vinaigrette salad dressing

Strawberries

Individual sponge cakes, or angel food cake

Jarred lemon curd

Sourdough rolls

from your pantry

Olive oil cooking spray

Cajun seasoning

Sugar

serves 4

beforeyoustart

In a large saucepan, covered, bring the water to a boil over high heat to make the soup.

step	1	cook the **chicken gumbo soup**
step	2	make the **jarlsberg cheese and walnut salad**
step	3	prepare the **sponge cakes with lemon curd and strawberries**
step	4	serve

 Recipes calling for strawberries usually specify that the berries be rinsed and hulled—in that order. Here's why: If you hull the strawberries first—that is, pull off the stems and carve out the white cores—and then wash them, the hollows absorb excess water and the berries get mushy. To save time, don't bother to hull the berries. Simply pluck off the stems and halve.

"Gumbo is a festive soup, terrific for parties. This recipe is a breeze to double."

—minutemeals' chef Paul

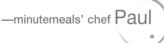

step 1

cook the **chicken gumbo soup**

1 pound skinless boneless chicken thighs, cut into 3/4 inch chunks

1 can (14.5 ounces) basil-, garlic-, and oregano-flavored diced tomatoes

1 package (10 ounces) frozen mixed soup vegetables or succotash

1 1/2 teaspoons Cajun seasoning

1 package (4 1/2 ounces) 10-minute boil-in-the-bag red beans and rice mix

1. Trim the fat from the chicken thighs and cut them into 3/4-inch chunks. Spray a large nonstick saucepan or Dutch oven with olive oil cooking spray. Place over medium-high heat, add the chicken, and cook 3 minutes or until lightly browned, turning once.

2. Meanwhile, bring 3 cups water to a boil, covered. Add the tomatoes, vegetable mixture, and Cajun seasoning.

3. Stir in the rice mixture and its seasoning packet. Bring to a simmer, cover, and cook 10 minutes, until the rice is tender and the chicken cooked through.

step 2

while the soup cooks, make the **jarlsberg cheese and walnut salad**

1/2 cup chopped walnuts

1 bag (10 ounces) prewashed European salad mix

4 slices (2 ounces) Jarlsberg cheese

1/4 cup balsamic vinaigrette salad dressing

1. Put the walnuts in a small skillet and toss over medium heat 2 to 3 minutes, until lightly toasted. Spread the nuts on a plate to cool.

2. Place the salad mix in a salad bowl. Cut the cheese crosswise into slivers and add to bowl.

step 3

prepare the **sponge cakes with lemon curd and strawberries**

1/2 pint fresh small strawberries

3 tablespoons sugar

4 individual sponge cakes, or 4 slices angel food cake

3/4 cup jarred lemon curd

1. Rinse the strawberries and hull. Halve the strawberries over and into a bowl, add the sugar, and toss to mix.

2. Place a sponge cake or slice of angel food cake on each of 4 dessert plates. Spoon the lemon curd into the hollows of the sponge cakes.

step 4

serve

1. Place the rolls in a napkin-lined basket and place on the table. Toss the salad with the dressing and walnuts and place it with 4 salad plates on the table.

2. Ladle the gumbo into 4 shallow bowls.

3. When ready for dessert, spoon some of the strawberries and their juice over the sponge cakes or angel food cake slices and serve.

Chicken Gumbo Soup
Single serving is 1/4 of total recipe
CALORIES 405; PROTEIN 29g; CARBS 45g;
TOTAL FAT 9g; SAT FAT 2g; CHOLESTEROL 77mg;
SODIUM 1265mg; FIBER 8g

sausage, bean, and escarole soup

italian salad

pesto garlic bread

ripe pears and hazelnut biscotti

menu gameplan

shopping list

Hot Italian pork sausage

Red kidney beans

Escarole

Roasted garlic–flavored chicken broth

Prepared garlic bread (from the refrigerator section)

Prepared pesto

Prewashed Italian salad mix

Jarred roasted red peppers

Ripe pears

Hazelnut biscotti

from your pantry

Olive oil cooking spray

Dried Italian herb blend

Grated Parmesan cheese

Extra virgin olive oil

Red wine vinegar

Salt and pepper

serves 4

beforeyoustart

Preheat the oven to warm the pesto garlic bread. Rinse the pears.

step 1 cook the **sausage, bean, and escarole soup**

step 2 prepare the **pesto garlic bread**

step 3 make the **italian salad**

step 4 serve

luckyforyou Whether it is spread on bread, or stirred into soups, sauces, and vinaigrettes, prepared pesto is real convenience food. If you don't use the prepared pesto here right away, freeze the remainder in ice cube trays, transferring the frozen cubes to self-sealing freezer bags. If you make your own, freeze the mixture before adding the Parmesan cheese—the flavor will be that much fresher when you add freshly grated cheese to the thawed pesto.

"I love the little kick from the hot sausage—if you prefer sweet, pass crushed red pepper flakes at the table."

—minutemeals' chef Paul

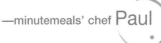

step 1

cook the **sausage, bean, and escarole soup**

12 ounces bulk hot Italian-style pork sausage

1 can (15 to 16 ounces) red kidney beans

1 head escarole (about 1 pound)

1 can (14.5 ounces) roasted garlic–flavored chicken broth

1 teaspoon dried Italian herb blend

1. Spray a deep nonstick skillet or Dutch oven with olive oil cooking spray and place it over medium-high heat. Crumble in the sausage and cook for 6 minutes, stirring occasionally and breaking up the meat with a spoon, until browned. Spoon off any excess drippings.

2. While the sausage browns, drain and rinse the kidney beans. Rinse the escarole and trim off any brown edges. Cut the escarole crosswise into 1-inch pieces. Add the beans and escarole to the sausage along with the chicken broth, Italian seasoning, and 2 cups water. Bring to a boil; cover, reduce the heat to medium, and simmer 10 minutes or until the escarole is just tender.

step 2

prepare the **pesto garlic bread**

1 loaf (about 1 pound) prepared garlic bread

1/3 cup prepared pesto

1. Preheat the oven according to the directions on the bread package. Split the bread lengthwise, if it is not already split. Pour off any excess oil from the pesto, and brush half the pesto on the cut sides of each half.

2. Bake the bread for the time suggested. Cut into slices using a serrated knife, place them in a napkin-lined basket, and cover to keep warm.

step 3

make the **italian salad**

1 bag (10 ounces) prewashed Italian salad mix

1 jar (7 ounces) roasted red peppers

1/4 cup grated Parmesan cheese

2 tablespoons extra virgin olive oil

1 tablespoon red wine vinegar

1. Place the salad mix in a serving bowl. Drain the peppers and tear them into pieces with your fingers, letting the pieces fall onto the greens.

2. Add the cheese, olive oil, vinegar, salt and pepper to taste, and toss. Place the salad on the table with salad plates for serving.

step 4

serve

1. Place the bread on the table. Ladle the hot soup into 4 bowls and serve at once.

2. When ready for dessert, serve the pears and the hazelnut biscotti.

Sausage, Bean, and Escarole Soup
Single serving is 1/4 of total recipe

CALORIES 230; PROTEIN 15g; CARBS 17g; TOTAL FAT 11g; SAT FAT 4g; CHOLESTEROL 34mg; SODIUM 949mg; FIBER 7g

in-a-manhattan-minute clam chowder

broccoli slaw

corn muffins with honey-pepper butter

apple pie ice cream

menu gameplan

shopping list

Thick-cut bacon

Precooked diced potatoes with onion (from the produce section)

Crushed tomatoes

Frozen mixed vegetables

Minced clams

Corn muffins

Prewashed broccoli, carrot, and cabbage slaw

Vanilla ice cream

Apple pie filling

from your pantry

Butter

Honey

Freshly ground black pepper

Ground cinnamon

Olive oil

Cider vinegar

Sugar

Salt

serves 4

beforeyoustart

Preheat the oven or toaster oven to 300°F to warm the corn muffins.

step 1 cook the **in-a-manhattan-minute clam chowder**

step 2 warm the **corn muffins** and make the **honey-pepper butter**

step 3 make the **broccoli slaw**

step 4 **serve**

luckyforyou

A good pair of kitchen shears can help you trim time from all sorts of kitchen tasks. We use them here to snip uncooked bacon (hence no cutting board to wash) and elsewhere in the book to snip fresh herbs.

"Even if you're loyal to creamy New England clam chowder, you'll love this Manhattan-style version. It's chunky, almost like stew."

—minutemeals' chef Patty

step 1

cook the **in-a-manhattan-minute clam chowder**

4 slices thick-cut bacon

1 bag (20 ounces) diced potatoes with onion

1 can (28 ounces) crushed tomatoes

1 bag (16 ounces) frozen mixed vegetables

2 cans (6 1/2 ounces each) minced clams

1. Snip the bacon into small strips with kitchen shears.

2. Place the bacon in a Dutch oven or large saucepan over high heat. Cook, stirring often, for 3 minutes, or until the bacon is crispy. Stir in the diced potatoes and onions and cook for 3 minutes, stirring often, until the potatoes start to brown.

3. Add the crushed tomatoes, frozen vegetables, and clams with their juices. Cover and bring to a boil. Reduce the heat to medium and simmer until the vegetables are heated and the flavors blended, about 10 minutes.

step 2

warm the **corn muffins** and make the **honey-pepper butter**

4 corn muffins

1/4 cup (1/2 stick) butter, softened

2 tablespoons honey

Pinch ground cinnamon

1. Preheat the oven or toaster oven to 300°F. Bake the corn muffins for 10 minutes until warmed through. Transfer the muffins to a napkin-lined basket and place on the table.

2. Combine the butter and honey in a small bowl and stir in a good grinding of black pepper and a pinch of cinnamon. Place on the table.

step 3

make the **broccoli slaw**

1/2 bag (16 ounces) broccoli, carrot, and cabbage slaw

2 tablespoons olive oil

1 tablespoon cider vinegar

Pinch sugar

In a large serving bowl toss the slaw mix with the olive oil, cider vinegar, sugar, and salt and pepper to taste. Place the bowl on the table.

step 4

serve

1. Divide the clam chowder among 4 soup bowls. Serve with the warm corn muffins, honey butter, and slaw.

2. When ready for dessert, scoop 1/2 cup vanilla ice cream into each of 4 dessert dishes. Top each serving with 1/4 cup apple pie filling, and sprinkle each with a dash of cinnamon.

In-a-Manhattan-Minute Clam Chowder
Single serving is 1/4 of total recipe (about 1 1/2 cups)

CALORIES 382; PROTEIN 24g; CARBS 60g; TOTAL FAT 6g; SAT FAT 2g; CHOLESTEROL 43mg; SODIUM 975mg; FIBER 12g

sweet pea soup
with mint
tabbouleh salad
with feta cheese
whole-wheat pita bread
lemon sorbet popsicles

menu
gameplan

serves 4

step **1** make the **sweet pea soup with mint**

step **2** assemble the **tabbouleh salad with feta cheese**

step **3** microwave the **whole-wheat pita bread**

step **4** **serve**

shopping list

Frozen peas

Fresh or dried mint leaves

Plain low-fat yogurt

Prepared tabbouleh salad

Crumbled feta cheese

Romaine lettuce

Whole-wheat pita bread

Lemon sorbet Popsicles

from your pantry

Fat-free reduced-sodium chicken broth

Sugar

Salt and pepper

headsup Tabbouleh, the Middle Eastern salad of bulgur wheat and fresh parsley dressed with lemon juice and olive oil, is available packaged in the refrigerator section, from your supermarket deli, or in specialty stores. Box mixes are available, too, but they take up to 30 minutes to prepare.

"This is soup for all seasons. In the spring, I make it with tender, fresh peas and serve it chilled."

—minutemeals' chef Hillary

step 1

make the **sweet pea soup with mint**

1 box (10 ounces) frozen peas

1 can (14$\frac{1}{2}$ ounces) fat-free reduced-sodium chicken broth

1 teaspoon sugar

1 tablespoon chopped fresh mint leaves or 1 teaspoon dried

$\frac{1}{4}$ cup plain low-fat yogurt

1. In a medium saucepan place the peas, chicken broth, sugar, and mint, if using dried. Cover and bring to a boil over high heat. Reduce the heat to medium and simmer 5 to 7 minutes, or until peas are very tender.

2. Purée the soup in batches in a blender or food processor until very smooth.

3. Return the purée to the saucepan and heat through over medium heat. Season to taste with salt and pepper. If you are using fresh mint, stir it into the soup.

step 2

assemble the **tabbouleh salad with feta cheese**

2 containers (8 ounces each) tabbouleh salad

4 ounces crumbled feta cheese

Romaine lettuce leaves

Place the tabbouleh salad in a medium serving bowl. Add the feta and toss gently. Place the bowl in the center of a large serving platter and arrange the romaine leaves around the bowl. Set the platter on the table with 4 salad plates.

step 3

microwave the **whole-wheat pita bread**

2 whole-wheat pita breads (6-inch diameter), halved

1. Wrap each of the pita halves in a sheet of paper towel and sprinkle the paper towel lightly with water.

2. Microwave the bread on High for 35 seconds, or until hot and steamy. Transfer the bread to a napkin-lined basket and place the basket on the table.

step 4

serve

1. Divide the soup among 4 soup bowls. Top each serving with a tablespoon of yogurt. Serve the soup with the tabbouleh salad and bread.

2. When ready for dessert, remove the Popsicles from the freezer and serve.

Sweet Pea Soup with Mint
Single serving is $\frac{1}{4}$ of total recipe

CALORIES 74; PROTEIN 5g; CARBS 12g; TOTAL FAT 1g; SAT FAT 0g; CHOLESTEROL 1mg; SODIUM 510mg; FIBER 4g

cream of spinach soup
rotisserie chicken with honey-mustard dipping sauce
french bread with sun-dried tomato tapenade
pineapple with mango sorbet

menu
gameplan

shopping list

Prewashed flat-leaf spinach

Heavy cream

French bread

Sun-dried tomato tapenade

Rotisserie chicken
(from the deli)

Light sour cream

Lime (for juice)

Pineapple chunks
(from the salad bar or
produce section, or
juice-packed canned)

Mango sorbet

from your pantry

Onion

Garlic

Fat-free reduced-sodium
chicken broth

Grainy Dijon mustard

Salt

Freshly ground black pepper

Honey

serves 4

beforeyoustart
Preheat the oven to 400°F to warm
the bread.

step **1** cook the **cream of spinach soup**

step **2** warm the **french bread**

step **3** make the **honey-mustard dipping sauce**

step **4** assemble the **pineapple with mango sorbet**

step **5** **serve**

headsup Puréeing hot soup—or any other hot food—in the blender can be tricky. Steam can build up, forcing the lid off of the blender and spraying hot food on both cook and kitchen. If you use a blender here to purée the soup, be sure to work in small batches, keeping your hand on the lid and venting it occasionally to let the steam escape as you work.

"After a busy day, I'd rather somebody else roast the chicken. Homemade soup lets me put my stamp on dinner." —minutemeals' chef Hillary

step 1
cook the **cream of spinach soup**

1 medium onion, sliced

2 small cloves garlic, crushed

2 cans (14½ ounces each) fat-free reduced-sodium chicken broth

2 packages (6 ounces each) prewashed flat-leaf spinach

½ cup heavy cream

1. Slice the onion. Crush the garlic cloves by smashing them with the flat side of a chef's knife.

2. Place the onion, garlic, and chicken broth in a large saucepan or Dutch oven; cover, and bring to a boil over high heat. Reduce the heat to medium and simmer 3 minutes.

3. Add the spinach, cover, and cook 3 minutes until wilted and lightly cooked. Purée the soup in batches in a food processor or blender until smooth.

4. Return the soup to the cooking pot and add the cream. Bring the soup just to a boil, covered, over medium heat. Season to taste with salt and freshly ground black pepper.

step 2
warm the **french bread**

1 loaf crusty French bread

1 jar (8 ounces) prepared sun-dried tomato tapenade

1. Preheat the oven to 400°F. Place the bread directly on the oven rack and heat for 3 to 5 minutes. Cut the bread into serving pieces, transfer them to a napkin-lined basket, and cover to keep warm.

2. Spoon the tapenade into a small bowl and place on the table.

step 3
make the **honey-mustard dipping sauce**

1 rotisserie chicken, cut into serving pieces

for the dipping sauce

⅓ cup grainy Dijon mustard

¼ cup light sour cream

2 tablespoons honey

2 tablespoons lime juice

1. Arrange the chicken on a serving platter.

2. In a small bowl combine the mustard, sour cream, honey, and lime juice. Place the dip and the chicken on the table.

step 4
assemble the **pineapple with mango sorbet**

2 cups pineapple chunks

1 pint mango sorbet

Divide the pineapple chunks evenly among 4 dessert bowls and refrigerate.

step 5
serve

1. Ladle the soup into 4 bowls and bring the bowls to the table. Place the bread on the table, and let diners pass the tapenade for spreading. Pass the chicken and the dipping sauce.

2. When ready for dessert, top each serving of pineapple with a scoop of sorbet and serve.

Cream of Spinach Soup
Single serving is ¼ of total recipe
CALORIES 134; PROTEIN 4g; CARBS 6g; TOTAL FAT 11g; SAT FAT 7g; CHOLESTEROL 41mg; SODIUM 751mg; FIBER 2g

speedy creamy carrot soup

watercress and red onion salad

cheesy boboli

quick ambrosia

menu
gameplan

beforeyoustart

Preheat the oven to 450°F to bake the Boboli.

step	1	cook the **speedy creamy carrot soup**
step	2	bake the **cheesy boboli**
step	3	make the **watercress and red onion salad**
step	4	assemble the **quick ambrosia**
step	5	**serve**

shopping list

Shredded carrots

Heavy cream

Thin-crust Boboli

Fontina or Swiss cheese

Watercress

Ginger-, sesame-, or soy sauce–flavored vinaigrette salad dressing

Sour cream, light or regular

Sweetened flaked coconut

from the salad bar

Red onion slices

Pineapple chunks (from produce department, or juice-packed canned)

Mandarin oranges (or juice-packed canned)

from your pantry

Fat-free reduced-sodium chicken broth

Ground ginger

Salt

White pepper

Grated Parmesan cheese

Italian herb mix

Crushed red pepper flakes

Brown sugar

luckyforyou Between the salad bar and produce section, supermarkets offer a wide variety of cut-up fruit that saves you from washing, peeling, and cutting. Use the time saved to focus on presentation: Create a beautiful mixed salad or composed fruit platter; roast or grill the fruit for an intriguing condiment or dessert.

"This menu strikes just the balance I was seeking. Sharp cheese, creamy soup, bitter greens, soothing dessert. They make sense together."

—minutemeals' chef Patty

step 1

cook the **speedy creamy carrot soup**

1 bag (10 ounces) shredded carrots

2 cups fat-free reduced-sodium chicken broth

1/2 cup heavy cream

1/2 teaspoon ground ginger

1. Place the carrots and 1/4 cup water in a large microwave-safe dish. Cover with a lid or vented plastic wrap and microwave on High for 8 minutes, stirring after 4 minutes, until carrots are tender. Remove the carrots from the microwave and let rest 2 minutes.

2. Transfer the cooked carrots to a blender or food processor. Pour in the chicken broth and purée until smooth. Transfer the mixture to a bowl or saucepan and stir in the heavy cream, ginger, and salt and pepper to taste. Heat in the microwave or on the stovetop until steaming hot.

step 2

bake the **cheesy boboli**

1 (10-ounce) thin-crust Boboli

1 cup shredded fontina or Swiss cheese

1/4 cup grated Parmesan cheese

1/2 teaspoon dried Italian herb mix

1/4 teaspoon crushed red pepper flakes

1. Preheat the oven to 450°F. Line a baking sheet with foil. Set the Boboli on the prepared sheet.

2. Coarsely shred the fontina cheese and sprinkle it over the Boboli. Top with the Parmesan cheese. Scatter the Italian herbs and red pepper flakes on top. Bake for 10 minutes, or until the cheese is bubbly.

step 3

make the **watercress and red onion salad**

1 bunch watercress

3 tablespoons ginger-, sesame-, or soy sauce–flavored vinaigrette salad dressing

1/2 cup red onion slices

1. Trim the woody stems from the watercress. Wash it thoroughly and spin dry.

2. Place the salad dressing in a serving bowl. Mound the watercress and red onion slices on top. Do not toss. Place the bowl on the table with 4 salad plates.

step 4

assemble the **quick ambrosia**

1/2 cup light or regular sour cream

2 tablespoons packed brown sugar

1 1/2 cups pineapple chunks, drained if canned

1 1/2 cups mandarin oranges, drained if canned

2 tablespoons sweetened flaked coconut

1. Mix the sour cream and brown sugar in a serving bowl.

2. Drain the pineapple chunks and mandarin oranges if using canned. Add the fruit to the sour cream mixture and toss until coated. Sprinkle with the coconut. Chill until serving time.

step 5

serve

1. Divide the carrot soup among 4 soup bowls.

2. Place the cheesy Boboli on a cutting board and bring it to the table with a pizza wheel. Toss the salad, and serve it on the 4 salad plates with wedges of the Boboli.

3. When ready for dessert, divide the ambrosia among 4 bowls and serve.

Speedy Creamy Carrot Soup
Single serving is 1/4 of total recipe
CALORIES 139; PROTEIN 2g; CARBS 9g;
TOTAL FAT 11g; SAT FAT 7g; CHOLESTEROL 41mg;
SODIUM 501mg; FIBER 2g

santa fe chicken salad

baked corn tortillas with salsa

margarita sundaes

menu gameplan

serves 4

shopping list

Thin-sliced chicken cutlets

Prewashed spring mix salad greens

Haas avocado

Brianna's Special Request Santa Fe Blend or Catalina salad dressing

Corn tortillas

Salsa

Limes (for juice)

Margarita mix

Strawberries

Lime or orange sorbet or sherbet

from your pantry

Cooking spray

Chili powder

Salt and pepper

Vegetable oil

Kosher salt

beforeyoustart

Preheat the broiler for the chicken. Chill glasses for dessert.

step **1** cook the **santa fe chicken salad**

step **2** bake the **corn tortillas**

step **3** assemble the **margarita sundaes**

step **4** **serve**

luckyforyou The conventional advice for pitting avocados really works: Halve the avocado, hold the pit half in your palm, insert a sharp knife blade (the edge, not the tip) into the pit, and twist. The pit will stick to the knife blade when you pull it out.

"On special occasions, I substitute shrimp for the chicken. It's an easy change that makes things feel a little fancier."

—minutemeals' chef Hillary

step 1

cook the **santa fe chicken salad**

1 1/2 teaspoons chili powder

1 pound thin-sliced chicken cutlets

2 bags (5 ounces each) spring mix salad greens

1 medium ripe Haas avocado

1/4 cup Brianna's Special Request Santa Fe Blend Salad Dressing, or Catalina

1. Preheat the broiler. Line a broiler pan with aluminum foil. Spray a broiler-pan rack with cooking spray. Stir together the chili powder, 1 teaspoon salt, and pepper to taste in a small bowl. Sprinkle the mixture over both sides of each breast. Place the chicken breasts on the prepared rack and broil 3 to 4 inches from the heat for 4 to 5 minutes, turning once, until cooked through. Transfer the chicken to a plate and cool slightly. Cut into 1/4-inch-thick strips.

2. Place the spring greens in a salad bowl. Halve, pit, and peel the avocado, cut it into cubes, and add to the salad.

step 2

bake the **corn tortillas**

4 corn tortillas (6-inch diameter)

2 teaspoons vegetable oil

Kosher salt

1 cup salsa

1. Reduce the oven heat to 400°F. Line 1 or 2 baking sheets with aluminum foil.

2. Brush the tortillas with the oil. Stack them and cut the stack into eight wedges. Arrange the wedges on the prepared baking sheets, sprinkle with salt, and bake 5 to 7 minutes, or until crispy.

step 3

assemble the **margarita sundaes**

2 limes

1/2 cup margarita mix

2 cups strawberries

1 pint lime sorbet or sherbet

1. Juice the limes. Combine the juice with the margarita mix and place in the refrigerator.

2. Rinse the strawberries, hull, and slice.

step 4

serve

1. Toss the chicken with the salad and the dressing. Divide evenly among 4 dinner plates.

2. Place the tortillas on the table in a napkin-lined basket or on a plate. Serve the salsa in a small bowl with the chips.

3. When ready for dessert, scoop the sorbet into each of 4 chilled glasses. Drizzle with the margarita-lime mix and the sliced strawberries.

Santa Fe Chicken Salad
Single serving is 1/4 of total recipe
CALORIES 287; PROTEIN 25g; CARBS 10g;
TOTAL FAT 16g; SAT FAT 3g; CHOLESTEROL 63mg;
SODIUM 893mg; FIBER 4g

couscous salad
with smoked turkey and nectarines
parmesan-walnut pitas
lemon mousse
with strawberries

menu gameplan

serves 4

shopping list

Mini pita breads

Chopped walnuts

Roasted garlic and olive oil couscous mix

Smoked turkey

Nectarines

Fresh mint

Olive oil and vinegar vinaigrette salad dressing, store-bought or homemade

Heavy cream

Lemon curd

Strawberries

from your pantry

Garlic

Butter

Shredded Parmesan cheese

Freshly ground black pepper

beforeyoustart

Preheat the oven to 400°F to toast the pitas. Chill a medium bowl and the beaters of an electric mixer for whipping the cream.

step 1 bake the **parmesan-walnut pitas**

step 2 make the **couscous salad with smoked turkey and nectarines**

step 3 assemble the **lemon mousse with strawberries**

step 4 serve

headsup
Supermarkets sell relatively small bunches of fresh mint—with just enough leaves for the ½ cup you'll need here. But if you buy a large bunch, here's the best way to keep it fresh: Stand the stems in water covered with a plastic bag secured to the container with a rubber band. It will keep in the refrigerator for a week or so if you change the water every other day.

"Please use fresh mint here—it really does make a difference and the green leaves are lovely against the nectarine slices." —minutemeals' chef Sarah

step 1

bake the **parmesan-walnut pitas**

4 mini pita breads
(3³/4 inch diameter)

1 clove garlic, halved
lengthwise

1 tablespoon butter, softened

2 tablespoons chopped
walnuts

¹/4 cup shredded Parmesan
cheese

1. Preheat the oven to 400°F. Place the pita breads on a baking sheet. Cut the garlic clove in half lengthwise.

2. Rub the tops of the pitas with the cut sides of the garlic. Spread the pitas with the butter and sprinkle with black pepper to taste, the walnuts, and Parmesan cheese. Bake until toasted, 6 to 8 minutes. Transfer to a plate or basket, and cover lightly to keep warm.

step 2

make the **couscous salad with smoked turkey and nectarines**

1 box (5.8 ounces) roasted garlic
and olive oil couscous mix

8 ounces smoked turkey
in one piece, cut into cubes

2 ripe nectarines, halved,
pitted, and sliced

¹/2 cup lightly packed mint
leaves, coarsely chopped

3 tablespoons olive oil and
vinegar vinaigrette salad dressing

1. Pour 1¹/4 cups water and the couscous seasoning packet into a medium saucepan, cover, and bring to a boil over high heat. Stir in the couscous. Cover and remove the pot from the heat; let stand 5 minutes.

2. Cut the turkey into cubes. Halve, pit, and slice the nectarines. Coarsely chop the mint. Fluff the couscous with a fork and turn into a large bowl.

3. Add the turkey, nectarines, mint, and salad dressing to the couscous. Toss to combine and set the bowl on the table.

step 3

assemble the **lemon mousse with strawberries**

¹/2 cup heavy cream

1 cup good-quality bottled
lemon curd

1 cup strawberries, hulled

1. In a chilled medium bowl, with an electric mixer on high speed, beat the cream until stiff.

2. Using a rubber spatula, fold the lemon curd into the whipped cream just until blended. Spoon the mousse into 4 dessert dishes.

3. Hull and thinly slice the strawberries. Top the mousse with the strawberries and refrigerate.

step 4

serve

1. Serve the salad with the toasted pitas.

2. For dessert, serve the mousse with strawberries.

**Couscous Salad with Smoked Turkey
and Nectarines**
Single serving is ¹/4 of total recipe

CALORIES 265; PROTEIN 17g; CARBS 43g;
TOTAL FAT 4g; SAT FAT 1g; CHOLESTEROL 24mg;
SODIUM 1000mg; FIBER 4g

shrimp and arugula salad with tomatoes

feta cheese and jalapeño spread

pumpernickel and crisp breads

pineapple chunks dipped in caramel sauce

menu gameplan

shopping list

Medium shrimp, cooked, peeled, and deveined

Brianna's Home Style Real French Vinaigrette Dressing, or good quality store-bought olive oil and vinegar salad dressing

Arugula or watercress

Grape or cherry tomatoes

Pitted kalamata or Gaeta olives

Fresh jalapeño pepper or canned chopped pickled jalapeño

Feta cheese

Sour cream, reduced-fat or regular

Crisp breads

Pumpernickel bread

Pineapple chunks (from the produce department or salad bar, or juice-packed canned)

Caramel apple dip

from your pantry

Salt

Freshly ground black pepper

Garlic

Extra virgin olive oil

serves 4

step **1** make the **shrimp and arugula salad with tomatoes**

step **2** make the **feta cheese and jalapeño spread**

step **3** serve

luckyforyou Any leftovers from the dessert here can be made into a quick breakfast treat: Just combine some pineapple and caramel sauce with yogurt, and whirl the trio in the blender for a delicious smoothie.

"Light and refreshing certainly doesn't have to mean bland. There's so much going on here, but nothing weighs you down."

—minutemeals' chef Lisa

step 1

make the **shrimp and arugula salad with tomatoes**

1 to 1¼ pounds cooked, peeled, and deveined medium shrimp

½ cup Brianna's Home Style Real French Vinaigrette Dressing

2 cups arugula or watercress, trimmed, rinsed, and spun dry

3 cups grape tomatoes, or stemmed cherry tomatoes

⅓ cup pitted kalamata or Gaeta olives

1. In a salad bowl, mix the shrimp, dressing, and salt and pepper to taste. Let marinate 10 minutes.

2. Meanwhile, trim, rinse, and dry the arugula or watercress. Place the arugula, grape tomatoes, and olives on top of the shrimp and set the bowl on the table with 4 salad plates. Do not toss.

step 2

make the **feta cheese and jalapeño spread**

1 small jalapeño pepper, seeded and diced, or 2 tablespoons drained, canned chopped pickled jalapeño

1 garlic clove

6 ounces feta cheese

3 tablespoons extra virgin olive oil

3 tablespoons reduced-fat or regular sour cream

1. Seed and dice the fresh jalapeño, if using. Place the jalapeño and the garlic in a food processor and process until finely chopped. Add the feta cheese and the olive oil and pulse until the mixture is almost smooth. Add the sour cream and pulse until combined.

2. Scrape the spread into a bowl and stir in salt and pepper to taste. Place the bowl on the table.

step 3

serve

1. Place the crisp and pumpernickel breads in a napkin-lined basket.

2. Toss the salad and serve it with the breads and feta-jalapeño spread.

3. When ready for dessert, put the pineapple chunks in one bowl and caramel sauce in another. Serve with toothpicks for dipping the pineapple into the caramel.

Shrimp and Arugula Salad with Tomatoes
Single serving is ¼ of total recipe

CALORIES 322; PROTEIN 26g; CARBS 12g; TOTAL FAT 19g; SAT FAT 3g; CHOLESTEROL 221mg; SODIUM 817mg; FIBER 2g

tuscan tuna and white bean salad

sliced tomatoes with basil

crusty cracked-wheat italian bread with dipping oil

honeyed grapes with lemon custard

serves 4

step 1 assemble the **tuscan tuna and white bean salad**

step 2 assemble the **sliced tomatoes with basil**

step 3 assemble the **honeyed grapes with lemon custard**

step 4 **serve**

shopping list

Canned tuna

Jarred marinated artichoke salad

Cannellini beans

Balsamic vinaigrette salad dressing, store-bought or homemade

Prewashed romaine salad mix

Tomatoes

Shallot

Fresh basil

Red grapes (from salad bar)

Slivered almonds

Custard-style lemon yogurt

Crusty cracked-wheat Italian bread

from your pantry

Salt and pepper

Extra virgin olive oil

Honey

Flavored olive oil

 Light tuna, especially imported Italian tuna packed in olive oil, is the most flavorful and tender of all the tuna varieties on the supermarket shelf. It is comparatively pricey, but you can frequently find it on sale—stock up when you do. If you prefer to save calories (and some money), you can substitute light or white tuna packed in water.

"This is a no-cook meal meant for a hot summer night, and it's a glorious spread."

—minutemeals' chef Sarah

step 1

assemble the **tuscan tuna and white bean salad**

2 cans (6 ounces each) light tuna in olive oil, drained

1 jar (12 ounces) marinated artichoke salad, drained

1 can (19 ounces) cannellini beans, drained and rinsed

2 tablespoons balsamic vinaigrette salad dressing

1 bag (10 ounces) prewashed romaine salad mix

Drain the tuna and the artichoke salad. Drain and rinse the cannellini beans. In a salad bowl, combine the beans, tuna, and artichoke salad with the dressing, stirring gently to avoid breaking up the tuna too much. Place the romaine salad mix on top of the tuna; do not toss. Refrigerate.

step 2

assemble the **sliced tomatoes with basil**

3 large ripe tomatoes (about 1¼ pounds)

1 shallot, peeled and chopped

1 tablespoon extra virgin olive oil

12 fresh basil leaves

1. Core and slice the tomatoes. Peel and chop the shallot.

2. Arrange the tomatoes on a serving platter. Sprinkle with the shallot, and salt and pepper to taste. Drizzle with the olive oil.

3. Stack the basil leaves and thinly slice. Sprinkle over the tomatoes. Place the platter on the table.

step 3

assemble the **honeyed grapes with lemon custard**

3/4 pound red grapes

1 tablespoon honey

2 tablespoons slivered almonds

2 containers (6 ounces each) custard-style lemon yogurt

1. Rinse the grapes and remove them from their stems. Combine the grapes and honey in a medium bowl.

2. Spread the almonds on a microwave-proof plate. Microwave on High 1 to 3 minutes, stirring frequently, until the almonds are toasted; tip them onto a plate to cool. Divide the grapes among 4 dessert dishes. Spoon the yogurt over the grapes.

step 4

serve

1. Pour the flavored olive oil into a small shallow bowl. Place the crusty Italian bread on a cutting board, and bring it to the table with the bowl of oil and a serrated knife. Let diners cut their own slices for dipping.

2. Gently toss the tuna, bean, and artichoke salad with the greens. Place the bowl on the table and serve with the tomatoes and the bread.

3. When ready for dessert, sprinkle the toasted almonds over the grapes and yogurt, and serve in 4 small bowls.

Tuscan Tuna and White Bean Salad
Single serving is ¼ of total recipe

CALORIES 346; PROTEIN 26g; CARBS 17g; TOTAL FAT 19g; SAT FAT 3g; CHOLESTEROL 13mg; SODIUM 802mg; FIBER 6g

panzanella
with bacon
lemon chicken soup
cocoa berries

menu
gameplan

shopping list

Crusty peasant bread

Bacon

Beefsteak tomatoes

Prewashed romaine
salad mix

Balsamic vinaigrette salad
dressing, store-bought or
homemade

Scallions

Lemon-and-herb-flavored
chicken broth

Sweetened condensed milk

Strawberries

from your pantry

Salt

Freshly ground black pepper

Olive oil

Sesame seeds

Unsweetened cocoa powder

Vanilla extract

serves 4

beforeyoustart

Preheat the broiler to toast the bread
and cook the bacon.

step **1** make the **panzanella with bacon**

step **2** heat the **lemon chicken soup**

step **3** make the **cocoa berries**

step **4** **serve**

heads up Thrifty cooks find a use for all
sorts of things that most of
us discard without a second thought. You can save and
refrigerate the bacon fat that gets rendered here, and use
a bit in place of oil or butter when you want to add a
smoky note to eggs, sautéed greens, chowder—just
about anything.

"When I have stale bread on hand, I skip the toasting step, making this salad even easier."

—minutemeals' chef Wendy

step 1
make the **panzanella with bacon**

1 small loaf crusty peasant bread (about 8 ounces)

8 ounces bacon

3 beefsteak tomatoes, cored and chopped

1 bag (10 ounces) prewashed romaine salad mix

1/3 cup balsamic vinaigrette salad dressing

1. Preheat the broiler. Line a baking sheet with foil. Tear the bread into large chunks. Place the bread on the prepared baking sheet and broil 6 inches from the heat for about 2 minutes, watching carefully, until toasted. Transfer the bread to a large salad bowl.

2. Place the bacon slices on the same baking sheet. Broil 6 inches from the heat for 7 to 8 minutes, turning once, until crisp. Drain bacon on paper towels. Crumble the bacon coarsely.

3. Core and coarsely chop the tomatoes, and add them to the bread. Add the romaine, bacon, dressing, and salt and pepper to taste; toss.

step 2
heat the **lemon chicken soup**

2 teaspoons olive oil

1 bunch scallions, thinly sliced

2 cans (14 1/2 ounces each) lemon-and-herb-flavored chicken broth

1 tablespoon sesame seeds

1. In a large saucepan, heat the olive oil over moderate heat.

2. Slice the scallions. Add the scallions to the saucepan and cook 1 minute to soften. Add the broth and bring to a boil, covered, over high heat. Remove from the heat and cover to keep warm.

step 3
make the **cocoa berries**

1 cup sweetened condensed milk

1/2 cup unsweetened cocoa powder

1 teaspoon vanilla extract

1 quart strawberries

In a small bowl, mix the condensed milk, cocoa powder, and vanilla until blended. Rinse the strawberries.

step 4
serve

1. Bring the panzanella to the table with 4 serving plates.

2. Ladle the soup into 4 bowls and sprinkle each serving with sesame seeds.

3. When ready for dessert, arrange the strawberries in a bowl. Place on the table with the sauce and 4 dessert plates, and let diners dip their berries.

Panzanella with Bacon
Single serving is 1/4 of total recipe

CALORIES 391; PROTEIN 13g; CARBS 39g; TOTAL FAT 21g; SAT FAT 5g; CHOLESTEROL 16mg; SODIUM 946mg; FIBER 4g

prosciutto, melon, and cheese salad

chilled mixed vegetable juice

country mixed-grain bread
with white bean "butter"

spumoni ice cream
with amaretti cookies

menu
gameplan

serves 4

beforeyoustart

Chill the mixed vegetable juice.

step 1 make the **white bean "butter"**

step 2 prepare the **prosciutto, melon, and cheese salad**

step 3 serve

shopping list

Cannellini beans

Cantaloupe or honeydew melon

Prewashed Italian salad mix

Thinly sliced prosciutto

Fontina or provolone cheese

Red wine vinaigrette salad dressing

Country-style mixed-grain bread

Mixed vegetable juice, such as V-8

Spumoni ice cream

Amaretti or wafer cookies

from your pantry

Garlic

Dried rosemary

Extra virgin olive oil

Salt

Freshly ground black pepper

 Prosciutto, the salted (not smoked) and air-cured ham, used to be available only in specialty stores. Affordable, domestically produced prosciutto is increasingly available from the deli sections of better supermarkets, but the sweet prosciutto di Parma (from the Italian city of Parma) is the gold standard. Prosciutto di San Daniele is another excellent option.

"I've served this menu for a light supper, lunch, and brunch. Whatever the time of day, it's surprising and elegant." —minutemeals' chef Paul

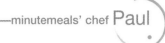

---

step 1

make the **white bean "butter"**

1 can (15 ounces) cannellini beans

1 garlic clove, peeled and crushed

1/4 teaspoon dried rosemary

1 tablespoon extra virgin olive oil

1. Drain the beans, reserving 2 to 3 tablespoons of the liquid. Peel the garlic clove and crush it with the flat side of a knife blade.

2. With the food processor running, drop the garlic clove and the rosemary through the feed tube; add the beans and olive oil and process until smooth, adding some of the reserved bean liquid if necessary to make a stiff but spreadable "butter."

3. Scrape the mixture into a small bowl. Season with salt and pepper to taste. If you like, drizzle a little more olive oil over the surface. Place the spread on the table.

---

step 2

prepare the **prosciutto, melon, and cheese salad**

1 large ripe cantaloupe or 1 medium honeydew melon

1 bag (10 ounces) prewashed Italian salad mix

4 ounces thinly sliced prosciutto (about 16 slices)

6 ounce chunk fontina or provolone cheese, cut into sticks

1/3 cup red wine vinaigrette salad dressing

1. Slice off the ends of the melon. Stand it on one cut end on a cutting board. With a sharp knife, slice from top to bottom to remove the rind. Halve the melon lengthwise, and scoop out the seeds. Slice each half into 4 wedges and halve the wedges crosswise.

2. Divide the salad greens among 4 dinner plates. Arrange the melon slices on top of the greens. Ruffle the prosciutto slices and drape them over the melon, dividing evenly. Cut the cheese into sticks and divide among plates. Grind some fresh pepper over each serving. Place the salad on the table with the dressing.

---

step 3

serve

1. Pour the glasses of chilled mixed vegetable juice. Put the bread in a napkin-lined basket and serve with the white bean "butter."

2. Serve the salad, passing the dressing.

3. When ready for dessert, serve slices of spumoni with the amaretti cookies.

Prosciutto, Melon, and Cheese Salad
Single serving is 1/4 of total recipe
CALORIES 380; PROTEIN 21g; CARBS 19g;
TOTAL FAT 25g; SAT FAT 11g; CHOLESTEROL 68mg;
SODIUM 1,417mg; FIBER 3g

steak salad
with hummus
corn muffins with cream cheese and hot pepper jelly
strawberries with sour cream and brown sugar

shopping list

Flank steak

Prewashed baby greens mix

Grape or cherry tomatoes

Red onion slices
(from the salad bar)

Hummus

Corn muffins

Low-fat cream cheese

Hot pepper jelly

Strawberries

Sour cream, reduced-fat
or regular

from your pantry

Salt

Freshly ground black pepper

Brown sugar

serves 4

beforeyoustart

Preheat the broiler to cook the steak.

step **1** make the **steak salad with hummus**

step **2** assemble the **corn muffins**

step **3** make the **strawberries with sour cream and brown sugar**

step **4** **serve**

lucky**for**you

If your supermarket doesn't carry pepper jelly, a favorite condiment in the American South, it's easy enough to make your own version of the sweet-spicy mixture: Simply stir 1/2 teaspoon of cayenne pepper into 1/2 cup orange marmalade.

"This menu is a global stew! Middle Eastern hummus, Southern pepper jelly—the flavors truly work together."

—minutemeals' chef **Wendy**

step 1

make the **steak salad with hummus**

- 1 beef flank steak (about 1¼ pounds), trimmed
- 1 bag (10 ounces) prewashed baby greens mix
- 1 pint grape tomatoes, or cherry tomatoes, stemmed
- ¼ cup red onion slices
- 8 ounces prepared hummus

1. Preheat the broiler. Line a broiler pan with aluminum foil. Place the flank steak on the broiler pan and season with salt and freshly ground black pepper to taste. Broil 4 inches from the heat for 10 minutes, turning once, until medium-rare.

2. Meanwhile, arrange the greens, grape tomatoes, and onion slices on a serving platter.

3. Thinly slice the steak on the diagonal, reserving any juices. Arrange the steak slices on top of the greens.

4. In a small bowl, combine the hummus and the reserved steak juices. If the mixture is too thick to pour, stir in a tablespoon of water. Drizzle the hummus over the steak and greens. Season with salt and pepper.

step 2

assemble the **corn muffins with cream cheese and hot pepper jelly**

- 4 corn muffins
- 1 container (8 ounces) soft low-fat cream cheese
- ½ cup hot pepper (jalapeño) jelly

Place the corn muffins in a basket, the cream cheese on a small plate, and the jelly in a small bowl, and set them on the table.

step 3

make the **strawberries with sour cream and brown sugar**

- 1 pint strawberries, rinsed and hulled
- ¾ cup reduced-fat or regular sour cream
- 2 tablespoons packed brown sugar

1. Rinse and hull the strawberries, and slice them into a serving bowl.

2. In a small bowl mix the sour cream and brown sugar. Place the mixture in the refrigerator until serving time.

step 4

serve

1. Place the salad on the table. Serve the salad with corn muffins, passing the cream cheese and hot pepper jelly.

2. When ready for dessert, divide the sliced strawberries among 4 dessert bowls and pass the sweetened sour cream for topping.

Steak Salad with Hummus
Single serving is ¼ of total recipe
CALORIES 360; PROTEIN 36g; CARBS 16g;
TOTAL FAT 17g; SAT FAT 5g; CHOLESTEROL 73mg;
SODIUM 469mg; FIBER 6g

curried egg salad pitas

spinach salad with grape tomatoes

bread-and-butter pickles

fruit juice spritzers

mango melba

menu
gameplan

shopping list

Curry paste

Pita breads

Grape or cherry tomatoes

Honey-Dijon salad dressing

Prewashed baby spinach

Pumpkin or sunflower seeds

Lime

Cranberry juice

Lime seltzer

Bread-and-butter pickles

Mango slices (bottled, from the produce department)

Lemon or mango sorbet

Pourable raspberry all-fruit

from the salad bar

Hard-cooked eggs

Shredded carrots

Mushroom slices

from your pantry

Mayonnaise

Salt and pepper

serves 4

beforeyoustart

Chill the cranberry juice and seltzer for the fruit juice spritzers.

step 1 prepare the **curried egg salad pitas**

step 2 assemble the **spinach salad with grape tomatoes**

step 3 make the **fruit juice spritzers**

step 4 serve

headsup

Thai cooking is built on curry pastes. The three basic pastes—red, green, and yellow—are heady mixtures of chile peppers, ginger, lemongrass, lime, and, depending on the color, cinnamon, coriander, turmeric, or other spices, and herbs.

"It's exciting to transform a simple, familiar dish like egg salad, just by stirring in an unexpected ingredient."

—minutemeals' chef Patty

step 1

prepare the **curried egg salad pitas**

6 hard-cooked eggs

1/2 cup shredded carrots

1/3 cup mayonnaise

1/2 teaspoon curry paste

4 pita breads (6-inch diameter)

1. Cut the eggs with an egg slicer and then coarsely chop. Stir in the shredded carrots, mayonnaise, and curry paste; season with salt and pepper.

2. Slit open or trim a slice off the pita breads. Carefully spoon 1/4 of the egg salad mixture into each of the pitas.

step 2

assemble the **spinach salad with grape tomatoes**

1 cup grape or cherry tomatoes, halved

1/3 cup honey-Dijon salad dressing

1 bag (5 ounces) prewashed baby spinach

1 cup mushroom slices

3 tablespoons pumpkin or sunflower seeds

Halve the grape or cherry tomatoes. Pour the dressing into a salad bowl. Add the spinach, mushrooms, and tomatoes, and pumpkin seeds. Do not toss.

step 3

make the **fruit juice spritzers**

1 lime

2 cups chilled cranberry juice

2 cups chilled lime seltzer

Cut 4 wedges from the lime. Pour 1/2 cup cranberry juice into each of 4 tall ice-filled glasses. Top each with 1/2 cup seltzer. Add a lime wedge to each.

step 4

serve

1. Toss the salad. Serve the sandwiches and salad with the bread-and-butter pickles and fruit juice spritzers.

2. When ready for dessert, place 4 mango slices in each of 4 dessert bowls. Scoop 1/2 cup lemon or mango sorbet over the mango slices and top with 1/4 cup pourable raspberry all-fruit.

Curried Egg Salad Pitas
Single serving is 1/4 of total recipe
CALORIES 418; PROTEIN 15g; CARBS 36g;
TOTAL FAT 23g; SAT FAT 5g; CHOLESTEROL 329mg;
SODIUM 682mg; FIBER 2g

minute
5-ingredient

poultry menus

meals
main dishes

sweet 'n tangy chicken breasts

raisin and nut coleslaw

crisp cheese breadsticks

pineapple cubes
with raspberry sorbet

shopping list

Skinless boneless
chicken breast halves

Orange marmalade

Chili sauce

Prepared coleslaw
(from the deli counter)

Green pepper slices
(from the salad bar)

Chopped walnuts

Crisp cheese breadsticks

Pineapple cubes
(from the salad bar
or produce department,
or juice-packed canned)

Raspberry sorbet

from your pantry

Nonstick cooking spray

Salt and pepper

Red or white wine vinegar

Dried basil

Raisins

serves 4

beforeyoustart

Preheat the broiler to cook the chicken
breasts. Chill the pineapple.

step	1	cook the **sweet 'n tangy chicken breasts**
step	2	assemble the **raisin and nut coleslaw**
step	3	warm the **crisp cheese breadsticks**
step	4	**serve**

luckyforyou
Skinless boneless chicken breasts are frequently on sale, sometimes in bulk family packs. When they are, double (or even triple) this recipe, refrigerate or freeze the portions you're not serving immediately, and then use them for a fast start on a tasty chicken salad, or to tuck into a picnic basket or brown-bag lunch.

"There are touches of sweetness throughout this menu, but the sweetest part may be how little cleanup the meal requires."

—minutemeals' chef Ruth

step 1

cook the **sweet 'n tangy chicken breasts**

4 skinless boneless chicken breast halves (about 1 1/2 pounds)

1/3 cup orange marmalade

3 tablespoons chili sauce

1 tablespoon red or white wine vinegar

3/4 teaspoon dried basil

1. Preheat the broiler. Line a broiler pan with aluminum foil and spray with nonstick cooking spray. Arrange the chicken breasts smoothest side down on prepared pan and season with salt and pepper to taste.

2. Place the marmalade, chili sauce, vinegar, and basil in a small bowl and mix well. Spread half of the marmalade mixture over the chicken breast halves.

3. Broil chicken about 6 inches from the heat for 5 minutes. Turn breasts and spread with remaining marmalade mixture. Broil 5 minutes longer or until glaze is bubbly and breasts are cooked through. (Note: Watch chicken carefully, and if browning too fast, reduce broiler heat or move to a lower shelf.)

4. Transfer the cooked chicken breasts to serving plates, spooning any pan juices over chicken.

step 2

assemble the **raisin and nut coleslaw**

2 cups coleslaw

1/2 cup green pepper slices

1/4 cup chopped walnuts

3 tablespoons raisins

Place coleslaw in a serving bowl. Coarsely chop the green pepper. Add the green pepper, walnuts, and raisins to the coleslaw. Mix well.

step 3

warm the **crisp cheese breadsticks**

1 package (about 4 ounces) crisp cheese breadsticks

Place breadsticks in a single layer on a small baking sheet. When chicken is finished broiling, turn off oven and warm the breadsticks for about 3 minutes while plating the chicken. (Or heat the breadsticks in a toaster oven.) Place the breadsticks in a napkin-lined basket.

step 4

serve

1. Divide the chicken breasts among 4 dinner plates.

2. Place the coleslaw and the breadsticks on the table.

3. When ready for dessert, arrange the pineapple cubes in 4 dessert dishes. Top with scoops of sorbet.

Sweet 'n Tangy Chicken Breasts
Single serving is 1/4 of total recipe
CALORIES 262; PROTEIN 35g; CARBS 21g;
TOTAL FAT 4g; SAT FAT 1g; CHOLESTEROL 94mg;
SODIUM 414mg; FIBER 0g

chicken cutlets
with chipotle mayonnaise
rice and beans
pudding hot chocolate

menu
gameplan

serves 4

step **1** cook the **rice and beans**

step **2** make the **chicken cutlets with chipotle mayonnaise**

step **3** make the **pudding hot chocolate**

step **4** **serve**

shopping list

Black beans

Thin-sliced chicken cutlets

Ground chipotle chile powder

Avocados

Lime (for juice)

Semisweet mini chocolate chips

from your pantry

Long-grain white rice

Chili powder

Salt and pepper

Vegetable spray

Mayonnaise

Cornstarch

Milk

Vanilla extract

headsup Chipotle peppers are jalapeño peppers that have been dried and smoked. They are available whole, canned in adobo sauce (a pungent mix of chiles, herbs, and vinegar), and powdered. If your supermarket doesn't carry the powder (check the McCormick spice selections) substitute a bit of canned pepper, diced, or combine chili powder with cayenne to taste.

"Adding herbs or spices to mayonnaise is the easiest way to stay ahead of the 'this again?' sandwich complaint."

—minutemeals' chef Wendy

step 1

cook the **rice and beans**

1 can (15 to 16 ounces) black beans

1 cup long-grain white rice

2 teaspoons chili powder

1. Drain the beans and place them in a medium microwave-safe bowl along with 2 cups water, rice, chili powder, and 1/2 teaspoon salt.

2. Cover with a lid and microwave on High for 20 minutes, until the rice is tender and the water has been absorbed.

step 2

make the **chicken cutlets with chipotle mayonnaise**

1 1/2 pounds thin-sliced chicken cutlets

1/2 cup mayonnaise

1/2 teaspoon ground chipotle chile powder

2 ripe avocados

1 lime

1. Season the chicken with salt and pepper to taste. Coat a large non-stick skillet with vegetable spray. Cook the chicken over medium-high heat 5 minutes, turning once, until cooked through. Transfer the chicken to a serving platter and keep warm.

2. In a small bowl stir together the mayonnaise and chipotle chile powder until smooth. Stir in any chicken juices that have accumulated on the platter.

3. Cut the avocados in half and remove the pits. With a spoon, scoop the flesh into a small serving bowl. Halve the lime, squeeze the juice over the avocado, and mash with a fork to achieve a chunky texture. Season with salt.

step 3

make the **pudding hot chocolate**

3 tablespoons cornstarch

3 cups milk

1 cup semisweet mini chocolate chips

1 teaspoon vanilla extract

1. In a small bowl whisk the cornstarch with 1/4 cup milk.

2. In a heavy medium saucepan over medium-high heat bring the remaining 2 3/4 cups milk, covered, just to a boil. Remove from the heat, add the chocolate chips, and stir until the chips are melted and the mixture is smooth.

3. Reduce the heat to medium and return the milk and chocolate mixture to the stove. Whisking constantly, add the cornstarch mixture to the chocolate mixture. Bring to a boil. Remove from the heat and stir in the vanilla. Cover surface with plastic wrap to prevent a skin from forming; do not refrigerate.

step 4

serve

1. Stir and fluff the rice and beans and bring to the table.

2. Divide the chicken cutlets evenly among 4 dinner plates. Pass the chipotle mayonnaise and the avocado.

3. When ready for dessert, divide the pudding among 4 dessert cups and serve.

Chicken Cutlets with Chipotle Mayonnaise
Single serving is 1/4 of total recipe

CALORIES 545; PROTEIN 37g; CARBS 9g;
TOTAL FAT 41g; SAT FAT 7g; CHOLESTEROL 110mg;
SODIUM 397mg; FIBER 5g

chicken cutlets
with apples and leeks
maple-and-spice winter squash
whole-grain rolls
frozen yogurt with bananas and caramel sauce

menu
gameplan

shopping list

Frozen puréed winter
(butternut) squash

Leeks

Apples

Thin-sliced chicken cutlets

Light cream

Dulce de leche frozen yogurt
or ice cream

Banana

Caramel sauce

Whole-grain rolls

from your pantry

Maple syrup

Butter

Pumpkin pie spice

Salt

Freshly ground black pepper

serves 4

step **1** cook the **maple-and-spice winter squash**

step **2** make the **chicken cutlets with apples and leeks**

step **3** prepare the **frozen yogurt with bananas and caramel sauce**

step **4** **serve**

headsup When we call for cooking
apples, we're looking for
varieties that retain their shape when cooked and whose
tartness will balance the sweet leeks and rich cream in the
sauce. Sweet-tart Jonagolds, Jonathans, and Macouns,
or the very tart Granny Smith fit the bill.

"This is a perfect meal for family and friends. The fragrance of warm apples and cinnamon makes people feel cared for." —minutemeals' chef Paul

step 1

cook the **maple-and-spice winter squash**

1 package (10 ounces) frozen puréed winter (butternut) squash

2 tablespoons maple syrup

1 tablespoon butter

1/2 teaspoon pumpkin pie spice

1. Cook the squash in the microwave according to the directions on the package.

2. Stir in the maple syrup, butter, and pumpkin pie spice; microwave 30 seconds longer. Stir and cover to keep warm.

step 2

while squash cooks, make the **chicken cutlets with apples and leeks**

2 leeks (about 12 ounces), trimmed, sliced, and rinsed

2 firm cooking apples, halved and thinly sliced

2 tablespoons butter

4 thin-sliced chicken cutlets (about 1 pound)

1/2 cup light cream

1. Fill a salad spinner, with the spinning basket inserted, with cold water. Trim the root and most of the green tops from the leeks, slice crosswise, and drop the slices into the water. Swish the leeks with your hand to dislodge any dirt. Lift out the basket, pour out the water, and then spin the leeks dry. Cut the apples in half through the cores and remove the cores with a melon baller. Thinly slice the apples.

2. Melt 1 tablespoon of the butter in a 12-inch nonstick skillet over medium-high heat. Add the chicken and cook for 3 to 4 minutes, turning once, until light golden and cooked through. Transfer the chicken to a platter.

3. While the chicken cooks, melt the remaining 1 tablespoon butter in another large skillet over medium heat. Add the leeks and cook, stirring occasionally, until they begin to soften, about 2 minutes. Add the apples and spread them in a single layer. Cover and cook 3 minutes.

4. Stir in the cream, 3/4 teaspoon salt, and 1/2 teaspoon pepper. Bring to a simmer. Cover and cook 2 to 3 minutes more, or until the apples are softened but still retain their shape. Remove from the heat and keep warm.

step 3

prepare the **frozen yogurt with bananas and caramel sauce**

1 pint dulce de leche frozen yogurt or ice cream

1 large banana, peeled and sliced

1/2 cup caramel sauce

Scoop the frozen yogurt or ice cream into 4 dessert dishes. Peel and slice the banana, and top each serving with some of the banana slices. Place the dishes in the freezer. Place the caramel sauce in a microwave-safe measure.

step 4

serve

1. Stir any juices from the chicken into the leek and apple sauce. Place a cutlet on each of 4 serving plates and spoon some of the sauce on top, dividing evenly. Spoon some of the squash next to each cutlet and serve.

2. Place the whole-grain rolls in a napkin-lined basket.

3. When ready for dessert, heat the caramel sauce in the microwave for 30 seconds. Drizzle some hot sauce over the bananas and frozen yogurt or ice cream and serve.

Chicken Cutlets with Apples and Leeks
Single serving is 1/4 of total recipe

CALORIES 300; PROTEIN 25g; CARBS 18g;
TOTAL FAT 15g; SAT FAT 8g; CHOLESTEROL 98mg;
SODIUM 512mg; FIBER 3g

grilled chicken
with green chile sauce

yellow rice with scallions
ranch-hand salad
lime-marinated watermelon with blackberries

shopping list

Skinless boneless chicken breast halves

Diced green chiles

Heavy cream

Taco seasoning

Fresh cilantro

Boil-in-the-bag yellow rice mix

Tomato

Scallion

Vidalia or other sweet white onion

Radishes

Prewashed salad greens

Peppercorn ranch salad dressing

Lime (for juice)

Cubed watermelon (from the salad bar or produce department)

Blackberries

from your pantry

Salt and pepper

Butter

Sugar

serves 4

beforeyoustart

Bring the water to a boil in a medium saucepan, covered, over high heat to cook the rice.

step	1	cook the **grilled chicken with green chile sauce**
step	2	cook the **yellow rice with scallions**
step	3	make the **ranch-hand salad**
step	4	assemble the **lime-marinated watermelon with blackberries**
step	5	**serve**

luckyforyou
Keeping an envelope of taco seasoning mix on hand gives you a quick way to add Tex-Mex flavor to foods without measuring out individual spices.

"Color inspired this menu as much as flavor did. Its hues—yellow, pink, purple—are as tropical as its taste."

—minutemeals' chef Sarah

step 1

cook the **grilled chicken with green chile sauce**

4 skinless boneless chicken breast halves (about 5 ounces each)

1 can (4 ounces) diced green chiles, rinsed and drained

1/2 cup heavy cream

1 tablespoon taco seasoning (from a packet)

1/2 cup cilantro leaves, chopped

1. Heat a nonstick grill pan over medium heat until hot. Season the chicken breasts with a total of 1/4 teaspoon each salt and pepper.

2. Pan-grill the chicken breasts, 4 to 5 minutes per side, or until cooked through.

3. While the chicken cooks, rinse and drain the chiles. In a 2-cup glass measure, stir together the chiles, cream, and taco seasoning. Microwave on High, 3 to 5 minutes, or until the sauce is hot and slightly thickened. While the sauce cooks, chop the cilantro. Stir the cilantro into the hot sauce.

step 2

cook the **yellow rice with scallions**

1 box (4 ounces) 10 minute boil-in-the-bag yellow rice mix

1 small tomato, diced

1 scallion, chopped

1 1/2 teaspoons butter

1. Bring 4 cups of water to a boil in a medium covered saucepan. Measure out 2 tablespoons water and set aside.

2. Place the rice pouch in the boiling water and cook for 10 minutes. Dice the tomato and chop the scallion.

3. Remove the rice pouch with tongs or a fork and let drain. Pour off the water from the saucepan. In the same saucepan, over low heat, combine the reserved 2 tablespoons water, the butter, and the seasoning packet from the rice mix; melt the butter. Open the rice pouch and stir the rice, tomato, and scallion into the melted butter. Remove from the heat and cover to keep warm.

step 3

make the **ranch-hand salad**

1/2 cup Vidalia or other sweet white onion slices (1 onion)

3 radishes

1 package (10 ounces) prewashed salad greens

1/4 cup peppercorn ranch salad dressing

1. Halve the onion, peel it, and slice enough to measure 1/2 cup. Rinse and slice the radishes.

2. Put the salad greens, the onion slices, and the radish slices into a salad bowl. Add the dressing and toss.

step 4

assemble the **lime-marinated watermelon with blackberries**

1/2 tablespoon fresh lime juice (1 lime)

2 tablespoons sugar

3 cups cubed watermelon

1 cup blackberries

1. Halve the lime and squeeze enough juice to measure 1 tablespoon juice.

2. Combine the lime juice and sugar in a medium bowl; stir to moisten the sugar. Add the watermelon and toss to coat. Refrigerate until serving time.

step 5

serve

1. Divide the chicken among 4 dinner plates and spoon the sauce over. Spoon some rice next to each serving of chicken. Serve with the salad.

2. When ready for dessert, add the blackberries to the watermelon and toss gently to avoid crushing the berries. Spoon the fruit with its syrup into 4 dessert dishes (use wine or martini glasses if you have them or at least glass dishes, to show off the colors) and serve.

Grilled Chicken with Green Chile Sauce
Single serving is 1/4 of total recipe
CALORIES 267; PROTEIN 29g; CARBS 3g;
TOTAL FAT 14g; SAT FAT 8g; CHOLESTEROL 119mg;
SODIUM 482mg; FIBER 1g

chicken and sugar-snap peas
with cream sauce
jasmine rice pilaf
very green salad
tin roof sundaes

menu
gameplan

serves 4

beforeyoustart
Bring 3½ cups water to boil in a medium saucepan, covered, over high heat to cook the rice.

step	1	cook the **jasmine rice pilaf**
step	2	cook the **chicken and sugar-snap peas with cream sauce**
step	3	prepare the **very green salad**
step	4	**serve**

shopping list

Lemon-Flavor Herb with Jasmine Rice Pilaf (Knorr brand)

Thin-sliced chicken cutlets

Heavy cream

Frozen sugar-snap peas

Broccoli florets (from the salad bar)

Cooked green beans (from the salad bar)

Balsamic vinaigrette salad dressing, store-bought or homemade

Prewashed mixed baby greens

Vanilla ice cream

Chocolate ice cream sauce

Salted roasted peanuts

from your pantry

Butter

Salt and pepper

Flour

Cooking spray

Dried tarragon

luckyforyou
Dusting the chicken with flour helps it to brown nicely. As a bonus, the flour also thickens the cream sauce, eliminating any time you would need to spend reducing the cream to thicken it.

"Cream sauce sounds unlikely for a minutemeal, but this simple sauce really works and tastes luxurious."

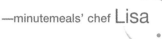

—minutemeals' chef Lisa

step 1

cook the **jasmine rice pilaf**

2 packages (5.1 ounces each) Lemon-Flavor Herb with Jasmine Rice Pilaf (Knorr brand)

2 tablespoons butter

1. Pour $3^{1}/_{2}$ cups water into a medium saucepan, cover, and bring to a boil over high heat. Add the rice and butter and return to a boil.

2. Reduce the heat to low, cover, and simmer for 15 minutes, until the rice is tender. Remove from heat.

step 2

cook the **chicken and sugar-snap peas with cream sauce**

1 pound thin-sliced chicken cutlets

2 tablespoons flour

$^{2}/_{3}$ cup heavy cream

$^{1}/_{2}$ teaspoon dried tarragon, crumbled

1 package (9 ounces) frozen sugar-snap peas

1. Season both sides of the chicken with salt and pepper to taste and dust with flour.

2. Spray a large nonstick skillet with cooking spray and place over medium-high heat. Add the chicken and cook until golden, turning once, 3 to 4 minutes.

3. Stir the heavy cream and tarragon into the skillet. Reduce heat to medium. When the cream comes to a boil, reduce heat to low. Gently stir in sugar-snap peas and season with salt and pepper. Cover and remove from heat. Let stand for 3 to 4 minutes.

step 3

prepare the **very green salad**

1 cup broccoli florets

1 cup cooked green beans

$^{1}/_{4}$ cup balsamic vinaigrette salad dressing

1 bag (6 ounces) prewashed mixed baby greens

In a salad bowl, toss the broccoli and green beans with the balsamic vinaigrette. Place the baby greens on top; do not toss. Put the bowl on the table.

step 4

serve

1. Fluff the rice with a fork and place on the table.

2. Arrange the chicken and sugar-snap peas down the center of a serving platter. Spoon the sauce down the center of the chicken and place the platter on the table. Serve the chicken with the rice and salad.

3. When ready for dessert, scoop the vanilla ice cream into 4 dishes and top with chocolate sauce and salted peanuts.

Chicken and Sugar-Snap Peas with Cream Sauce
Single serving is $^{1}/_{4}$ of total recipe
CALORIES 302; PROTEIN 26g; CARBS 10g; TOTAL FAT 18g; SAT FAT 10g; CHOLESTEROL 117mg; SODIUM 222mg; FIBER 2g

flat but flavorful grilled chicken

red and green salad

garlic bread

cheesecake with blueberry topping

menu gameplan

serves 4

shopping list

Fresh oregano

Skinless boneless chicken breast halves

French bread

Cherry tomatoes (from the salad bar)

Prewashed mixed spring or baby greens

Italian salad dressing

Cheesecake with blueberry topping

from your pantry

Salt and pepper

Extra virgin olive oil

Garlic-flavored olive oil

beforeyoustart

Preheat the oven to 400°F to warm the garlic bread. Preheat the grill, if using.

step	1	marinate and cook the **flat but flavorful grilled chicken**
step	2	make the **garlic bread**
step	3	assemble the **red and green salad**
step	4	**serve**

luckyforyou Pounding chicken evens out its thickness and also tenderizes it. Sometimes, though, it's a step in a recipe that no one wants to undertake. In that case, buy thin-sliced chicken cutlets. Just be careful not to overcook them on the grill. Some cutlets can be paper-thin.

"The fresh, clean flavors of this menu were inspired by a trip to northern Italy."

—minutemeals' chef Nancy

step 1

marinate and cook the **flat but flavorful grilled chicken**

2 tablespoons chopped fresh oregano

4 skinless boneless chicken breast halves (about 1¼ pounds total)

2 tablespoons extra virgin olive oil

1. Preheat the grill, if using. Chop enough oregano to measure 2 tablespoons.

2. If the butcher cannot flatten the chicken breasts for you, place 1 between 2 large pieces of plastic wrap. With a wooden rolling pin or meat mallet, gently pound the breast to an even ¼-inch thickness. Repeat with the remaining 3 chicken breasts. Season on both sides with salt and pepper to taste.

3. In a pie plate, combine the olive oil and oregano. One at a time, add the pounded chicken breasts and turn to coat with the herbed oil. Stack the chicken in the marinade and let marinate while you move onto making the garlic bread.

4. To grill the chicken: Place the chicken breasts on the heated grill or grill pan and cook the first side until you can see the meat on the sides of the breast begin to turn opaque and the breast has grill marks, about 3 minutes, depending upon how hot the grill is. Turn and grill another 3 to 4 minutes, about 5 to 7 minutes total cooking time. Remove from the heat to prevent overcooking.

step 2

make the **garlic bread**

1 small loaf of French bread

2 tablespoons garlic-flavored olive oil

1. Preheat the oven to 400°F.

2. Slice the loaf in half horizontally. Brush the cut sides with the flavored olive oil and sprinkle with salt to taste. Place, cut side up, on a cookie sheet and heat until golden brown, about 7 to 10 minutes.

step 3

assemble the **red and green salad**

1 pint ripe cherry tomatoes

1 bag (5 ounces) prewashed mixed spring or baby greens

¼ cup Italian salad dressing

1. Rinse the tomatoes and pat dry. Halve, if desired.

2. Place the greens in a bowl, add the tomatoes and dressing, and toss.

step 4

serve

1. Mound ¼ of the salad on each of 4 dinner plates and lay a grilled chicken breast on top.

2. Slice the garlic bread, place in a bread basket, and place on the table.

3. When ready for dessert, cut the cheesecake into slices and serve.

Flat but Flavorful Grilled Chicken
Single serving is ¼ of total recipe

CALORIES 200; PROTEIN 29g; CARBS 0g; TOTAL FAT 9g; SAT FAT 0g; CHOLESTEROL 75mg; SODIUM 85mg; FIBER 0g

chicken and artichoke stir-fry

curly noodles

grated carrot and pear salad

orange sorbet with raspberries

menu
gameplan

shopping list

Scallions

Canned artichoke hearts, packed in water

Thin-sliced chicken cutlets

Stir-fry sauce

Sliced or shredded radishes (from the salad bar)

Lemons (for juice)

Pear

Shredded carrots (from the produce department)

Japanese chuka soba noodles

Orange sorbet or ice milk

Raspberries

from your pantry

Vegetable cooking spray

Vegetable oil

Sugar

Salt

Freshly ground black pepper

serves 4

beforeyoustart
Bring water to a boil in a large pot, covered, over high heat to cook the noodles. Rinse the pear.

step **1** cook the **chicken and artichoke stir-fry**

step **2** make the **grated carrot and pear salad**

step **3** cook the **curly noodles**

step **4** **serve**

 Chuka soba, the Japanese curly egg noodles used in ramen soup mixes, (other soba noodles are made from buckwheat) are easier to prepare than rice—no need to measure either noodles or cooking water. Look for KA-ME brand dried chuka soba at your supermarket, or, if you can't find them, substitute 2 packages of ramen soup noodles, cooking them according to the package directions and omitting the seasoning packet.

"Use chopsticks to eat the noodles. Sure, it makes for some silliness at the table, but that's not a bad thing."

—minutemeals' chef Lisa

cook the **chicken and artichoke stir-fry**

2 bunches scallions, trimmed, cut into 1-inch pieces

1 can (13.75 ounces) artichoke hearts packed in water, very well drained, halved

1¼ pounds thin-sliced chicken cutlets, cut into strips

¾ cup stir-fry sauce

½ cup sliced or shredded radishes

1. Trim the scallions and cut on the diagonal into 1-inch pieces. Drain the artichoke hearts and cut each heart in half. Place the scallions and artichokes in a large bowl.

2. Cut the chicken into thin strips and add to the vegetables. (Leaving the chicken for last means you only have to wash the cutting board once.)

3. Spray a large, deep nonstick pan with cooking spray. Place the pan over medium-high heat. Add the chicken mixture and cook, tossing frequently, about 8 minutes, until the chicken is cooked through. Add the stir-fry sauce and cook, stirring often, until hot and bubbly, about 2 minutes.

step 2

make the **grated carrot and pear salad**

3 tablespoons lemon juice (1 or 2 lemons)

2 teaspoons vegetable oil

1 teaspoon sugar

1 firm pear

1 package (10 ounces) shredded carrots

1. Squeeze enough fresh lemon juice to measure 3 tablespoons. In a serving bowl, stir together the lemon juice, the vegetable oil, and the sugar.

2. Grate the pear on the coarse side of the grater, grating around all sides and discarding the core. Add the grated pear and the carrots to the bowl, and toss gently to mix. Season with salt and freshly ground black pepper to taste, toss, and place on the table with 4 salad plates.

step 3

cook the **curly noodles**

2 packages (5 ounces each) Japanese chuka soba noodles

1. Bring a large pot of water to a boil, covered, over high heat. Just before the stir-fry finishes cooking, drop the noodles into the boiling water.

2. When the noodles rise to the top of the water, stir and let cook 4 to 5 minutes.

3. Drain noodles and divide among 4 large, shallow bowls.

step 4

serve

1. Divide the stir-fry among the 4 bowls of noodles. Sprinkle each serving with some of the radishes and place on the table with the salad.

2. When ready for dessert, scoop the orange sorbet into 4 bowls, sprinkle with the raspberries, and serve.

Chicken and Artichoke Stir-Fry
Single serving is ¼ of total recipe

CALORIES 281; PROTEIN 33g; CARBS 22g; TOTAL FAT 8g; SAT FAT 1g; CHOLESTEROL 78mg; SODIUM 297mg; FIBER 10g

chicken curry

rice with spinach

tomato, cucumber, and vidalia onion salad

pound cake with orange-honey sauce

menu
gameplan

shopping list

Instant brown rice

Prewashed spinach
(from the salad bar)

Kirby cucumbers

Tomato

Vidalia or other sweet
white onion

Lemon (for juice)

Chicken tenders

Coconut milk

Fresh cilantro

Vanilla yogurt

Pound cake

from your pantry

Salt

Freshly ground black pepper

Curry powder

Vegetable oil

Orange juice

Honey

serves 4

step	1	make the **rice with spinach**
step	2	make the **tomato, cucumber, and vidalia onion salad**
step	3	make the **chicken curry**
step	4	make the **pound cake with orange-honey sauce**
step	5	**serve**

headsup We call for coconut milk here, not coconut cream; both are unsweetened, but the milk is more dilute and so not as rich as the cream. You can thin coconut cream with water and substitute it for the milk, but watch that you don't grab cream of coconut from the supermarket shelf—it is sweetened, and used mostly in beverages and desserts.

"Gussy up the curry for company. Pass raisins, shredded unsweetened coconut, and chutney, and let your guests choose what they like."

—minutemeals' chef Wendy

step 1

make the **rice with spinach**

- 2 cups instant brown rice
- 2 cups prewashed spinach

1. Cook the rice in a medium saucepan in the amount of water and for the time directed on the package.

2. Place the spinach in the bottom of a serving bowl. Mound the hot rice on top and mix well to wilt the spinach. Season with salt and freshly ground black pepper to taste and cover to keep warm.

step 2

make the **tomato, cucumber, and vidalia onion salad**

- 2 kirby cucumbers, halved and chopped
- 1 large ripe tomato, coarsely chopped
- 1 Vidalia or other sweet white onion, halved and sliced
- 1 lemon

1. Halve the cucumbers lengthwise and cut the halves into thick slices. Coarsely chop the tomato. Halve and slice the onion.

2. Combine the cucumbers, tomato, and onion in a serving bowl. Cut the lemon in half and squeeze the juice over the vegetables. Season with salt and pepper to taste and toss.

step 3

make the **chicken curry**

- 1 1/2 pounds chicken tenders
- 2 tablespoons curry powder
- 1 tablespoon vegetable oil
- 1 cup coconut milk
- 2 tablespoons fresh cilantro leaves

1. In a medium bowl toss the chicken with the curry powder and salt and pepper to taste until evenly coated.

2. In a large nonstick skillet, heat the oil over high heat. Add the chicken and cook 3 minutes, turning, until the pink color is almost gone.

3. Stir in the coconut milk. Cook 2 to 3 minutes, stirring often, until milk is slightly thickened and chicken is cooked through.

4. Transfer the chicken and sauce to a serving dish, sprinkle with cilantro leaves, and partially cover to keep warm.

step 4

make the **pound cake with orange-honey sauce**

- 8 ounces vanilla yogurt
- 1/4 cup orange juice
- 2 tablespoons honey
- 4 slices pound cake

In a small serving bowl stir together the yogurt, orange juice, and honey.

step 5

serve

1. Bring the rice, chicken, and salad to the table. Place a serving of rice on each of 4 dinner plates, and spoon some of the curry over. Pass the salad.

2. When ready for dessert, place a piece of cake on each of 4 dessert plates and serve with the orange-honey sauce.

Chicken Curry
Single serving is 1/4 of total recipe
CALORIES 335; PROTEIN 36g; CARBS 4g;
TOTAL FAT 20g; SAT FAT 12g; CHOLESTEROL 94mg;
SODIUM 237mg; FIBER 2g

buffalo chicken tenders

potato salad

cherry tomatoes and vegetable sticks with blue cheese dressing

carrot cake

menu
gameplan

serves 4

step **1** cook the **buffalo chicken tenders**

step **2** prepare the **cherry tomatoes and vegetable sticks**

step **3** plate the **potato salad**

step **4** **serve**

shopping list

Chicken tenders

Hot sauce, such as Frank's

Blue cheese salad dressing

Celery sticks, baby carrots (or carrot sticks), and cherry tomatoes (from the salad bar or produce department)

Potato salad

Carrot cake

from your pantry

Salt and pepper

Vegetable oil

Butter

 There's no need to limit yourself to mayonnaise-based potato salad. Supermarkets, delis, and gourmet stores offer potato salads dressed with vinaigrette or pesto, or that include roasted vegetables and herbs. Choose your favorite.

"Just make this once, and I bet you won't need a shopping list the next time—it's that easy."

—minutemeals' chef Patty

step 1

cook the **buffalo chicken tenders**

1¼ pounds chicken tenders

1 tablespoon vegetable oil

2 tablespoons melted butter

¼ cup hot sauce, such as Frank's

1. Season the chicken tenders with ¼ teaspoon salt and ⅛ teaspoon pepper.

2. Heat the oil in a large heavy non-stick skillet over medium-high heat. Add the chicken tenders and cook, turning often, for 7 to 8 minutes, or until the chicken is lightly browned and cooked through.

3. Meanwhile, melt the butter in a small saucepan over low heat. Stir in the hot sauce.

4. Add the hot sauce mixture to the skillet, reduce the heat to medium, and cook for an additional 2 minutes until the chicken tenders are coated and the sauce has been absorbed. Remove from the heat.

step 2

prepare the **cherry tomatoes and vegetable sticks with blue cheese dressing**

½ cup blue cheese salad dressing

Celery sticks

Baby carrots or carrot sticks

Cherry tomatoes

Pour the blue cheese dressing in a small bowl. Place the bowl on a serving dish and surround with the celery sticks, baby carrots, and cherry tomatoes.

step 3

plate the **potato salad**

1 pound store-bought potato salad

Transfer the potato salad to a serving bowl and place on the table.

step 4

serve

1. Divide the chicken among 4 dinner plates.

2. Place the vegetable platter on the table.

3. When ready for dessert, slice the carrot cake into individual portions, place on dessert plates, and serve.

Buffalo Chicken Tenders
Single serving is ¼ of total recipe
CALORIES 236; PROTEIN 29g; CARBS 1g;
TOTAL FAT 13g; SAT FAT 5g; CHOLESTEROL 94mg;
SODIUM 276mg; FIBER 0g

bbq chicken sloppy joes

spiced shoestring potatoes
tomato salad
dill pickle spears
mint chip ice cream

menu
gameplan

shopping list

Assorted color
cherry tomatoes

Red onion slices
(from the salad bar)

Fresh basil

Frozen shoestring potatoes

Ground chicken

Barbecue sauce

Hamburger rolls

Dill pickle spears

Mint chip ice cream

from your pantry

Olive oil

Balsamic vinegar

Salt

Freshly ground black pepper

Ground cumin

Paprika

Cayenne pepper

Chili powder

serves 4

beforeyoustart

Preheat the oven to 450°F to cook the spicy fries; chill the dill pickle spears.

step **1** assemble the **tomato salad**

step **2** cook the **spiced shoestring potatoes**

step **3** cook the **bbq chicken sloppy joes**

step **4** **serve**

headsup

Ground chicken is extremely lean. Unlike all but the leanest ground beef, it doesn't exude fat when sautéed, so you won't need to drain it before adding the sauce.

"It's Friday afternoon. You're tired. But the family dinner is important to you—this is the stress-free meal to make."

—minutemeals' chef David

step 1

assemble the **tomato salad**

2 pints assorted color cherry tomatoes

1/2 cup red onion slices

1/2 cup fresh basil leaves

3 tablespoons olive oil

2 tablespoons balsamic vinegar

1. Halve the cherry tomatoes. Combine the onion slices and tomatoes in a salad bowl.

2. Stack the basil leaves and slice them intro strips. Add the basil strips to the bowl. Add the oil and vinegar and toss gently. Season with salt and freshly ground black pepper to taste.

step 2

cook the **spiced shoestring potatoes**

4 cups (about 1/2 of a 28-ounce bag) frozen shoestring potatoes

2 teaspoons ground cumin

1 teaspoon paprika

Cayenne pepper to taste, optional

1. Preheat the oven to 450°F. Spread the shoestring potatoes on a baking sheet and bake 10 to 15 minutes.

2. Transfer the fries to a large bowl and toss with the cumin and paprika. Season to taste with cayenne pepper, if using, and salt. Keep warm.

step 3

cook the **bbq chicken sloppy joes**

1 tablespoon olive oil

1 pound ground chicken

2 teaspoons chili powder

1 cup prepared barbecue sauce

4 seeded hamburger rolls

1. Heat the oil in a large nonstick skillet over medium-high heat. Add the ground chicken and cook, stirring occasionally, 5 to 6 minutes, until the pink color is gone. Stir in the chili powder and cook 1 minute longer. Add the barbecue sauce and cook 2 to 3 minutes until thickened.

2. Place a hamburger bun bottom on each of 4 plates. Spoon some of the sloppy Joe mixture over each and top with the remaining bun halves.

step 4

serve

1. Serve the sloppy Joes with the spiced fries, tomato salad, and dill pickle spears.

2. When ready for dessert, scoop the mint chip ice cream into 4 bowls and serve.

BBQ Chicken Sloppy Joes
Single Serving is 1/4 of total recipe

CALORIES 312; PROTEIN 16g; CARBS 30g; TOTAL FAT 15g; SAT FAT 4g; CHOLESTEROL 77mg; SODIUM 789mg; FIBER 3g

chicken sausage and potato hash

broccoli with garlic

slaw with blue cheese

apple pie à la mode

menu
gameplan

serves 4

shopping list

Chicken sausage

Precooked diced potatoes with onion (from the produce department)

Pre-shredded coleslaw mix

Blue cheese salad dressing

Chopped walnuts

Apple pie

Vanilla ice cream

from the salad bar

Red or green pepper slices

Mushroom slices
(or from the produce department)

Broccoli florets
(or from the produce department)

from your pantry

Vegetable oil

Salt

Garlic

Crushed red pepper flakes

Butter

Pepper

beforeyoustart

Preheat the oven to 250°F to warm the apple pie.

step **1** cook the **chicken sausage and potato hash**

step **2** cook the **broccoli with garlic**

step **3** assemble the **slaw with blue cheese**

step **4** **serve**

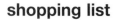

luckyforyou

Chicken sausage is available in a wide variety of flavors and quite a bit healthier than pork sausage: One chicken sausage has 149 calories and 11 grams of fat, compared to 216 calories and 17 grams of fat for pork. Even better, many worthy brands are available already fully cooked, so you just have to heat the sausage through before serving.

"Hash makes fine dinner fare. Serve it with just a green salad to save time—but don't skip the pie."

—minutemeals' chef Sarah

step 1
cook the **chicken sausage and potato hash**

2 tablespoons vegetable oil

1 pound fully cooked chicken sausage, cut into 1/2-inch thick slices

1 1/2 cups red or green pepper slices

1 bag (1 pound 4 ounces) precooked diced potatoes with onion

8 ounces mushroom slices

1. Heat the oil in a large, heavy skillet over medium-high heat. Slice the sausage and dice the red or green pepper slices.

2. Add the sausage, peppers, potato and onion mixture, mushrooms, and 1/4 teaspoon salt to the skillet. Cook, turning frequently with a spatula, until the potatoes are tender and lightly browned, 12 to 14 minutes.

step 2
cook the **broccoli with garlic**

4 cups broccoli florets

1 large garlic clove, crushed through a press

1/8 teaspoon crushed red pepper flakes

1 tablespoon butter

1. In a large microwave-safe dish, place the broccoli, 1/4 cup water, the garlic, red pepper flakes, and salt to taste.

2. Cover with a lid or vented plastic wrap and microwave on High 5 to 7 minutes, stirring once, or until the broccoli is crisp-tender. Add the butter, and cover to melt the butter and keep the broccoli warm.

step 3
assemble the **slaw with blue cheese**

2 cups pre-shredded coleslaw mix

3 tablespoons blue cheese salad dressing

3 tablespoons chopped walnuts

Combine the coleslaw mix, dressing, and walnuts in a serving bowl. Season with salt and pepper to taste. Toss and refrigerate until serving.

step 4
serve

1. Preheat the oven to 250°F. Place the pie in the oven to warm during dinner.

2. Toss the broccoli to coat with the butter, and serve it with the sausage and potatoes, and the slaw.

3. When ready for dessert, serve wedges of the warm pie topped with scoops of vanilla ice cream.

Chicken Sausage and Potato Hash
Single serving is 1/4 of total recipe
CALORIES 452; PROTEIN 22g; CARBS 36g; TOTAL FAT 25g; SAT FAT 6g; CHOLESTEROL 91mg; SODIUM 1106mg; FIBER 5g

turkey cutlets
with spinach and feta
mashed potatoes with horseradish and chives
angel food cake with raspberry sorbet and sauce

menu
gameplan

shopping list

Thin-sliced turkey breast cutlets

Prewashed spinach

Garlic-and-herb flavored feta cheese

Prepared mashed potatoes (from the refrigerated section of the produce department)

Chives (or chopped scallions, from the salad bar)

Seedless raspberry jam

Angel food cake

Raspberry sorbet

from your pantry

Olive oil

Salt and pepper

Garlic

Butter

Horseradish

serves 4

| step | 1 | make the **turkey cutlets with spinach and feta** |

| step | 2 | make the **mashed potatoes with horse-radish and chives** |

| step | 3 | prepare the **angel food cake with raspberry sorbet and sauce** |

| step | 4 | **serve** |

luckyforyou
Now that garlic-and-herb flavored, crumbled feta is available in supermarkets, you can get those flavors quickly and easily—no chopping necessary.

"I used assertive flavors throughout this menu without sacrificing the comfort factor or simplicity—you'll love it."

—minutemeals' chef Paul

make the **turkey cutlets with spinach and feta**

2 tablespoons olive oil

1 pound thin-sliced turkey breast cutlets

1 bag (10 ounces) prewashed spinach

2 cloves garlic, chopped

3/4 cup crumbled garlic-and-herb flavored feta cheese

1. In a large skillet, heat 1 tablespoon of the oil over medium-high heat. Add the turkey cutlets, seasoning them with 1/4 teaspoon each salt and pepper as they cook. Cook for 3 to 5 minutes, turning once, until golden and cooked through. Transfer to a plate and tent loosely with foil to keep warm.

2. Heat the remaining 1 tablespoon oil in the skillet. Add half of the spinach and the garlic; cook, tossing with 2 spoons until wilted. Add the remaining spinach and cook, tossing, until all of the spinach is wilted and any liquid is almost evaporated. Stir in the feta cheese and cook 1 minute more. Spread the spinach and feta mixture on a serving platter and lay the turkey cutlets on top, slightly overlapping, down the center. Pour any juices from the turkey over the top.

step 2

while the cutlets cook, make the **mashed potatoes with horseradish and chives**

1 package (20 ounces) prepared mashed potatoes

1 tablespoon butter

3 tablespoons chopped chives or scallions

2 tablespoons prepared horseradish

1. Peel back the plastic cover on the potatoes, leaving one side attached. Cut up the butter into small bits and scatter over the potatoes. If using chives, snip enough to measure 3 tablespoons over the top of the potatoes, or scatter the scallions over. Re-cover the potatoes with the plastic.

2. Microwave on High for 2 minutes. Stir the horseradish into the potatoes and microwave for 1 minute more.

step 3

prepare the **angel food cake with raspberry sorbet and sauce**

1/2 cup seedless raspberry jam

Angel food cake

1 pint raspberry sorbet

Place the jam in a small microwave-safe dish and put in the microwave.

step 4

serve

1. Season the mashed potatoes with salt and pepper to taste and bring to the table.

2. Place the platter of turkey cutlets on the table. Use a spatula to transfer a cutlet with some of the spinach to each of 4 dinner plates.

3. When ready for dessert, slice the cake and place a slice on each of 4 dessert plates. Top each slice with a scoop of sorbet. Heat the jam in the microwave for 30 seconds, stirring until smooth. Spoon some sauce around the cake slices and serve.

Turkey Cutlets with Spinach and Feta
Single serving is 1/4 of total recipe

CALORIES 298; PROTEIN 37g; CARBS 4g;
TOTAL FAT 15g; SAT FAT 6g; CHOLESTEROL 102mg;
SODIUM 615mg; FIBER 1g

thanksgiving on a roll

butternut squash

warm chocolate chip and caramel cookies

menu gameplan

shopping list

Refrigerated chocolate chip and caramel cookie dough (Nestlé)

Jarred turkey gravy

Sliced roast turkey (from the deli counter)

Turkey stuffing (Stovetop)

Kaiser rolls

Whole-berry cranberry sauce

Frozen butternut squash

Heavy cream

from your pantry

Butter

Salt

Ground nutmeg

serves 4

beforeyoustart

Preheat the oven to 350°F to bake the cookies. Bring 2 cups of water to a boil in a medium saucepan, covered.

step **1** bake the **warm chocolate chip and caramel cookies**

step **2** cook the **thanksgiving on a roll**

step **3** cook the **butternut squash**

step **4** **serve**

luckyforyou
The availability of prepared, refrigerated "break-apart" cookie dough makes it possible to have freshly baked cookies anytime.

"In the winter, this is a once-a-week menu for my family—sometimes even a warm weekend lunch."

—minutemeals' chef Patty

step 1

bake the **warm chocolate chip and caramel cookies**

1 package (18 ounces) refrigerated chocolate chip and caramel cookie dough (Nestlé)

1. Preheat the oven to 350°F.

2. Arrange the cookie dough on a baking sheet as directed on the package. Bake for 11 to 13 minutes. Cool on wire rack until time for dessert.

step 2

cook the **thanksgiving on a roll**

1 jar (12 to 16 ounces) turkey gravy

1 pound sliced roast turkey

1 package (6 ounces) turkey stuffing (Stovetop)

4 kaiser rolls

1 can (16 ounces) whole-berry cranberry sauce

1. Pour the gravy into a large non-stick skillet. Add the sliced turkey, cover, and heat gently over low heat.

2. Prepare the stuffing as directed on the package.

3. Meanwhile, split the rolls in half. When ready to serve, place a generous scoop of stuffing on each roll. Drape 1/4 of the turkey slices on top of each serving, and spoon some of the gravy over. Dollop some of the cranberry sauce on top, serving remaining cranberry sauce on the side.

step 3

cook the **butternut squash**

1 package (10 ounces) frozen butternut squash

2 tablespoons heavy cream

1 tablespoon butter

Pinch ground nutmeg

1. Bring 2 cups water to a boil in medium saucepan, covered, over high heat. Add the squash. Return to a boil, reduce the heat to medium, cover, and cook for 5 to 7 minutes, until the squash is tender.

2. Drain the cooked squash and return it to the saucepan. Using a potato masher, mash the squash with the cream, butter, salt to taste, and nutmeg. Transfer to a serving bowl.

step 4

serve

1. Place the turkey sandwiches on the table and serve with the remaining cranberry sauce and the squash.

2. When ready for dessert, place freshly baked cookies on a platter. Serve with glasses of milk, if desired.

Thanksgiving on a Roll with Cranberry Sauce
Single serving is 1/4 of total recipe
(with 1 tablespoon cranberry sauce)

CALORIES 629; PROTEIN 43g; CARBS 63g;
TOTAL FAT 22g; SAT FAT 5g; CHOLESTEROL 91mg;
SODIUM 1366mg; FIBER 5g

turkey burgers
with provolone and pesto
garlic-and-herb tossed fries
chopped vegetable salad
chocolate milkshakes

shopping list

Frozen shoestring potatoes

Salt-free garlic-and-herb seasoning

Ground turkey

Tomato

Refrigerated basil pesto

Sliced provolone cheese

Hamburger buns

Italian salad dressing

Chocolate ice cream

from the salad bar

Broccoli florets

Cauliflower florets

Red pepper slices

Crisp lettuce

from your pantry

Grated Parmesan cheese

Vegetable cooking spray

Salt and pepper

Milk

Chocolate syrup

serves 4

beforeyoustart

Preheat the broiler to cook the fries and the turkey burgers. Place the chocolate sauce in a saucepan of very hot water.

step	1	cook the **garlic-and-herb tossed fries**
step	2	cook the **turkey burgers with provolone and pesto**
step	3	assemble the **chopped vegetable salad**
step	4	make the **chocolate milkshakes**
step	5	**serve**

headsup
With turkey burgers, you only have one option for doneness: cooking until no traces of pink remain. If you can't judge from touch (the burgers should feel firm to the touch of your fingertip), insert a meat thermometer into the center of the burger after the recommended broiling time. The burgers are done when the thermometer reads 165°F.

"Everybody loves the classic cheeseburger and fries. Everybody loves Italian. So why not put them together? Now that's fusion cooking."

—minutemeals' chef Sarah

step 1
cook the **garlic-and-herb tossed fries**

4 cups (about 1/2 of a 28-ounce bag) frozen shoestring potatoes

1/2 teaspoon salt-free garlic-and-herb seasoning

2 tablespoons grated Parmesan cheese

1. Preheat the broiler. Spread the fries in a single layer in a jelly-roll pan.

2. Broil the fries 4 inches from the heat, until golden brown and crisp, turning occasionally with a spatula, 6 to 8 minutes. Sprinkle with the garlic-and-herb seasoning and Parmesan cheese. Broil until the cheese melts, about 1 minute longer, and remove from the heat.

step 2
cook the **turkey burgers with provolone and pesto**

1 pound ground turkey

1 large ripe tomato, sliced

3 tablespoons refrigerated basil pesto

4 slices provolone cheese

4 hamburger buns, split

1. Spray a broiler pan rack with cooking spray.

2. Mix the ground turkey with salt and pepper to taste and form into 4 flat patties. Place the burgers on the prepared rack and broil about 4 inches from the heat for 5 to 6 minutes, turning once, until cooked through. While the burgers cook, slice the tomato.

3. Spread the burgers with the pesto and top each with a slice of cheese. Broil until the cheese melts, about 1 minute longer. Top each burger with a tomato slice.

step 3
assemble the **chopped vegetable salad**

1 cup each broccoli florets, cauliflower florets, and red pepper slices

2 cups torn crisp lettuce

2 tablespoons Italian salad dressing

Coarsely chop the vegetables and the lettuce. Place in a salad bowl. Add the salad dressing, salt and pepper to taste, and toss to mix. Place the bowl on the table.

step 4
make the **chocolate milkshakes**

1 quart milk

1/2 cup chocolate syrup

4 scoops (about 1/2 cup each) chocolate ice cream

Place the milk and chocolate syrup in the blender container. Chill until ready for dessert. (Depending on your blender, you may need to make the shakes in 2 batches.)

step 5
serve

1. Serve the burgers on the buns, accompanied by the fries and salad.

2. When ready for dessert, add the ice cream to the blender and blend until the mixture is smooth and creamy; divide among 4 tall glasses and serve immediately.

Turkey Burgers with Provolone and Pesto
Single serving is 1/4 of total recipe
CALORIES 481; PROTEIN 35g; CARBS 26g;
TOTAL FAT 26g; SAT FAT 9g; CHOLESTEROL 106mg;
SODIUM 809mg; FIBER 2g

turkey falafel
meze platter
rice pudding with golden raisins

menu gameplan

shopping list

Plain low-fat yogurt

Hothouse cucumber

Precooked turkey meatballs

Hummus, plain or flavored

Whole-wheat pita bread pockets (6-inch diameter)

Grape tomatoes

Pepperoncini

Black or green olives

Feta cheese

Stuffed grape leaves

Golden raisins

Apple juice

Prepared rice pudding

from your pantry

Olive oil cooking spray

Salt and pepper

serves 4

beforeyoustart
Preheat the broiler to cook the turkey meatballs. Place the yogurt in a strainer to drain.

step 1 prepare the **turkey falafel**

step 2 compose the **meze platter**

step 3 make the **rice pudding with golden raisins**

step 4 **serve**

headsup
"Meze" is Greek for hors d'oeuvres. Luckily, the delicacies on the meze platter are not hard to find. If your supermarket doesn't carry some of them, make substitutions as needed.

"I adore New York City street-cart falafel. My adaptation is neat—it's much faster than making homemade or box-mix falafel."

—minutemeals' chef Hillary

step 1

prepare the **turkey falafel**

- 1 container (8 ounces) plain low-fat yogurt
- 1 cup diced hothouse cucumber
- 1 package (12 ounces) precooked turkey meatballs
- 4 ounces hummus, plain or flavored
- 2 whole-wheat pita bread pockets (6-inch diameter), halved

1. Preheat the broiler. Line a jelly-roll pan with aluminum foil.

2. Place the yogurt in a colander lined with a paper coffee filter or a sheet of paper towel to drain. Dice enough hothouse cucumber to measure 1 cup.

3. Cut each meatball in half. Arrange the meatballs, close together and cut side up, on the prepared jelly-roll pan. Spray the cut surfaces lightly with olive oil cooking spray. Broil the meatballs 6 inches from the heat for 3 minutes, until the tops are golden brown and crisp. Transfer to a medium bowl, add the hummus, and toss gently to coat. Cover loosely to keep warm.

4. When ready for dinner: Wrap the pita halves in a piece of paper towel and sprinkle lightly with water. Microwave on High for about 1 minute. When ready to serve, transfer the drained yogurt to a small bowl and stir in the cucumber. Season with salt and pepper to taste.

5. Tuck the meatballs into the warm pita halves and top with the yogurt and cucumber mixture.

step 2

compose the **meze platter**

- 1 pint grape tomatoes
- 1 jar (12 ounces) pepperoncini
- 8 ounces high-quality black or green olives, plain or marinated
- 1 thick slice (about 4 ounces) feta cheese
- 8 stuffed grape leaves

Place the grape tomatoes, pepperoncini, and olives in small bowls. Cut the feta cheese into rough chunks and place in a small bowl. Arrange the grape leaves on a plate. Place all of the meze on a large platter or directly on the table.

step 3

make the **rice pudding with golden raisins**

- 1/2 cup golden raisins
- 1/3 cup apple juice
- 16 ounces prepared rice pudding

1. Place the raisins and apple juice in a small saucepan. Bring to a boil, covered, over high heat. Remove from the heat and let cool.

2. Drain the juice from the raisins and stir them into the rice pudding. Divide among 4 dessert dishes. The pudding may be served warm; if you prefer it chilled, place the dessert dishes in the refrigerator.

step 4

serve

1. Serve the falafel with the meze.

2. When ready for dessert, serve the rice pudding.

Turkey Falafel
Single serving is 1/4 of total recipe
CALORIES 317; PROTEIN 26g; CARBS 33g; TOTAL FAT 10g; SAT FAT 2g; CHOLESTEROL 76mg; SODIUM 573mg; FIBER 5g

artichoke and white bean frittata

beet, apple, and watercress salad

sun-dried tomato pesto bread

fresh cherries with chocolate biscotti

menu gameplan

shopping list

Canned sliced small beets

Golden Delicious apple

Shallot

Honey-mustard or citrus vinaigrette salad dressing

Watercress

Whole-wheat Italian bread

Sun-dried tomato pesto

Jarred marinated artichoke hearts

Chives or scallions

Cannellini beans

Cherries

Chocolate biscotti

from your pantry

Salt

Freshly ground black pepper

Eggs

Olive oil

serves 4

beforeyou**start**

Turn the oven to 475°F to warm the bread and bake the frittata.

step 1 make the **beet, apple, and watercress salad**

step 2 bake the **sun-dried tomato pesto bread**

step 3 cook the **artichoke and white bean frittata**

step 4 serve

headsup To cut watercress easily, lay a bunch on its side and slice through the stems slightly below the point where the leaves begin to branch off; then wash and spin dry.

"You can top frittatas with whatever you like. Think of them as little egg pizzas, and feel free to experiment."

—minutemeals' chef Paul

step 1

make the **beet, apple, and watercress salad**

1 can (16 ounces) sliced small beets, drained

1 large Golden Delicious apple, thinly sliced

1 shallot, thinly sliced

1/4 cup honey mustard or citrus vinaigrette salad dressing

1 bunch watercress, trimmed and rinsed

1. Drain the beets and place in a medium bowl. Cut the apple into quarters, remove the core, and cut crosswise into thin slices. Peel and thinly slice the shallot. Add the apple and shallot slices to the beets. Add 3 tablespoons of the dressing, season with salt and pepper to taste, and toss to mix.

2. Trim, rinse, and spin dry the watercress. Spread it on a platter. Spoon the beet and apple mixture on top, and drizzle the remaining 1 tablespoon dressing over all. Place the salad on the table.

step 2

bake the **sun-dried tomato pesto bread**

1 pound loaf whole-wheat Italian bread

1/4 cup sun-dried tomato pesto

Turn the oven to 475°F. Split the loaf lengthwise almost all the way through, so that it opens like a book. Spread the pesto on the cut surfaces. Close, lay it attached-side-down, and slice at 1-inch intervals without cutting all the way through the attached side. Wrap the loaf in aluminum foil and place it in the oven.

step 3

cook the **artichoke and white bean frittata**

1 jar (about 6 ounces) marinated artichoke hearts, drained

6 large eggs

1/4 cup chopped chives or scallion greens

2 teaspoons olive oil

1 cup drained canned cannellini beans

1. Drain the artichokes, reserving the liquid. Coarsely chop the artichokes. Pour 3 tablespoons of the artichoke liquid into a medium bowl. Add the eggs, chives, 1/2 teaspoon salt, and 1/4 teaspoon pepper, and beat with a wire whisk until blended.

2. Place the oil in a large nonstick skillet with an oven-proof handle. (If the handle is not oven proof, wrap it in heavy-duty aluminum foil.) Heat the oil over medium heat. Add the egg mixture and cook, stirring occasionally, for 3 minutes. Scatter the artichokes and beans on top. Cover and cook 3 minutes longer or until the frittata is almost set.

3. Place the skillet in the upper third of the oven and bake for 2 to 4 minutes or until the frittata is set in center. Invert the frittata onto a serving plate.

step 4

serve

1. Carefully unwrap the bread and place it in a napkin-lined basket.

2. Using a pizza wheel or very sharp knife, cut the frittata into quarters and serve with the salad and bread.

3. When ready for dessert, rinse the cherries and serve them with the chocolate biscotti.

Artichoke and White Bean Frittata
Single serving is 1/4 of total recipe

CALORIES 222; PROTEIN 14g; CARBS 15g; TOTAL FAT 12g; SAT FAT 3g; CHOLESTEROL 319mg; SODIUM 681mg; FIBER 4g

minute

5-ingredient

meat menus

meals

main dishes

skillet beef
and orzo dinner
buttered peas
iceberg wedges
with russian dressing
fudgsicles

menu
gameplan

shopping list

Ground beef

Orzo

Shredded Mexican cheese mix

Frozen baby peas

Iceberg lettuce

Russian salad dressing

Fudgsicles

from your pantry

Salt and pepper

Ketchup

Butter

serves 4

beforeyoustart

Bring the water to a boil in a large pot, covered, over high heat, to cook the orzo. Preheat the broiler.

step **1** make the **skillet beef and orzo dinner**

step **2** make the **buttered peas**

step **3** assemble the **iceberg wedges with russian dressing**

step **4** **serve**

lucky**for**you
If you don't own an oven-proof skillet—that is, a skillet with a heat-proof handle—it's easy to make one with the equipment you have on hand: Just cover a conventional skillet handle with heavy-duty aluminum foil to protect it from the oven heat.

"My four-year-old loves to share. But when I suggested bringing this dish to a friend's house—no go."

—minutemeals' chef Wendy

step 1

make the **skillet beef and orzo dinner**

1½ pounds ground beef

⅓ cup ketchup

1 cup orzo

1 cup shredded Mexican cheese mix

1. Preheat the broiler. Bring 4 cups of water to a boil in a teapot.

2. Heat a large, deep skillet with an ovenproof handle over high heat. Crumble in the beef and season with salt and pepper to taste. Cook the meat, stirring occasionally to break up the chunks, until the pink color is gone, about 4 minutes. Transfer to a bowl and stir in the ketchup. Cover and keep warm.

3. In the same skillet, pour the boiling water and add a pinch of salt. Stir in the orzo and cover. Cook, stirring occasionally, until *al dente,* about 8 minutes. Drain.

4. Return the beef to the skillet. Spread the orzo evenly over the beef. Cover with the shredded cheese. Broil 4 inches from the heat for 2 minutes to melt the cheese.

step 2

make the **buttered peas**

1 box (10 ounces) frozen baby peas

2 teaspoons butter

Place the peas in a small saucepan with 2 tablespoons of water. Bring to a boil, cover, reduce the heat to medium, and simmer 4 to 5 minutes or until tender. Transfer the peas to a serving bowl using a slotted spoon, and toss with the butter and salt and pepper to taste. (Or cook the peas in the microwave according to the directions on the package, drain and toss with butter and salt and pepper.) Keep warm until ready to serve.

step 3

assemble the **iceberg wedges with russian dressing**

1 head iceberg lettuce

¼ cup Russian dressing

1. Core the lettuce by banging it, core-side down, on the counter. Twist the now-loosened core and pull out. Rinse, shake out any excess water, and pat dry with paper towels. Cut the lettuce head into quarters.

2. Place each quarter on a salad plate and spoon 1 tablespoon of dressing over.

step 4

serve

1. Bring the skillet dinner to the table and serve with the buttered peas and the salads.

2. When ready for dessert, pass out the Fudgsicles.

Skillet Beef and Orzo Dinner
Single serving is ¼ of total recipe
CALORIES 601; PROTEIN 45g; CARBS 38g; TOTAL FAT 29g; SAT FAT 13g; CHOLESTEROL 143mg; SODIUM 682mg; FIBER 1g

moroccan spiced beef patties

moroccan couscous
spinach with yogurt
pirouette cookies with cannoli dipping sauce

menu
gameplan

serves 4

shopping list

Lean ground beef

Mediterranean curry-flavored couscous

Prewashed microwave baby spinach

Plain low-fat yogurt

Whole-milk ricotta cheese

Orange marmalade

Chocolate-dipped roll cookies (pirouettes)

from your pantry

Pumpkin pie spice

Ground cumin

Salt and pepper

Sugar

Ground cinnamon

step **1** make the **moroccan spiced beef patties**

step **2** make the **moroccan couscous**

step **3** make the **spinach with yogurt**

step **4** make the **cannoli dipping sauce**

step **5** **serve**

luckyforyou We saved you the time needed to measure individual spices for the burgers by calling for pumpkin pie spice mix, a neat flavor trick for meat.

"I call these Kasbah burgers—my way of adding drama to the standard burger, without straying out of kid bounds." —minutemeals' chef Wendy

make the **morrocan spiced beef patties**

1 teaspoon pumpkin pie spice

3/4 teaspoon ground cumin

1 1/4 pounds lean ground beef

1. In a small heavy skillet, mix the pumpkin pie spice, cumin, and 1/4 teaspoon salt. Toast the spice mixture over medium heat, stirring constantly, until fragrant, about 1 minute.

2. Place the ground beef in a medium bowl and, using your hands, work in the toasted spice mixture, being careful not to over-mix. Shape the mixture into 4 slightly oval burgers, dividing evenly.

3. Heat a large, heavy skillet, preferably cast-iron, over medium-high heat. Cook the burgers for 8 to 10 minutes, turning once, until cooked through.

step 2

make the **moroccan couscous**

1 package (5.7 ounces) Mediterranean curry-flavored couscous

Make the couscous with the amount of water and for the time directed on the package.

step 3

make the **spinach with yogurt**

1 package (10 ounces) prewashed microwave baby spinach

1/4 cup plain low-fat yogurt

1. Microwave the spinach as directed on the bag.

2. Stir the yogurt into the spinach. Season with salt and pepper to taste. Cover lightly to keep warm.

step 4

make the **cannoli dipping sauce**

15 ounces whole-milk ricotta cheese

1/4 cup orange marmalade

2 tablespoons sugar

1/2 teaspoon ground cinnamon

In a food processor place the ricotta, marmalade, sugar, and cinnamon. Process about 45 seconds, scraping down the sides of the work bowl as needed, until the ricotta is smooth.

step 5

serve

1. Bring the burgers, spinach, and couscous to the table. Serve.

2. When ready for dessert, arrange the cookies on a platter and place on the table with the cannoli sauce and 4 dessert plates. Let diners dip their own cookies.

Moroccan Spiced Beef Patties
Single serving is 1/4 of total recipe

CALORIES 255; PROTEIN 27g; CARBS 1g; TOTAL FAT 15g; SAT FAT 6g; CHOLESTEROL 94mg; SODIUM 224mg; FIBER 0g

tortilla, beef, and bean bowl
ranch salad platter
coconut sorbet sundaes

serves 4

shopping list

Lean ground beef

Chili-hot beans

Avocado

Tortilla chips

Iceberg lettuce mix

Plum tomatoes

Kirby cucumbers

Vidalia or other sweet white onion

Peppercorn or regular Ranch salad dressing

Slivered almonds

Hot fudge sauce

Coconut sorbet

from your pantry

Chili powder

Pepper

step 1 make the **tortilla, beef, and bean bowl**

step 2 prepare the **ranch salad platter**

step 3 make the **coconut sorbet sundaes**

step 4 **serve**

 Most likely your refrigerator and pantry hold an array of fixings for the tortilla bowls. Shredded Cheddar or Monterey Jack cheese, thinly sliced fresh or canned diced jalapeño peppers, sour cream or yogurt, salsa—pass them all and let your diners top their tortilla bowls as they wish.

"I've substituted ground turkey or chicken, even sliced pork tenderloin, for the ground beef here. The flavor is always big."

—minutemeals' chef David

step 1

make the **tortilla, beef, and bean bowl**

12 ounces lean ground beef

1 1/2 tablespoons chili powder

1 can (15 to 16 ounces) chili-hot beans

1 avocado, peeled, pitted, and diced

4 cups small tortilla chips

1. Heat a large heavy skillet over medium-high heat. Add the ground beef and cook, stirring occasionally, until browned, 4 to 5 minutes. Drain off any fat and return the skillet to the heat. Stir in the chili powder and then the beans with their liquid and simmer 4 to 5 minutes. Remove from the heat.

2. Peel, pit, and dice the avocado. Stir into the beef mixture and season with pepper to taste. Cover and keep warm until serving time.

step 2

prepare the **ranch salad platter**

1 bag (16 ounces) iceberg lettuce mix

4 plum tomatoes, cut into wedges

2 kirby cucumbers, sliced into rounds

1/2 Vidalia or other sweet white onion, thinly sliced

1/3 cup peppercorn or regular Ranch salad dressing

Spread the salad mix on a large, deep platter. Cut the tomatoes into thin wedges, the cucumbers into rounds, and the onion into thin slices. Scatter the vegetables over the lettuce. Drizzle the salad with the dressing.

step 3

make the **coconut sorbet sundaes**

1/4 cup slivered almonds

1/2 cup hot fudge sauce

1 pint coconut sorbet

1. Spread the almonds on a microwave-proof plate. Microwave on High, 2 to 3 minutes, stirring frequently, until the almonds are toasted; tip them onto a plate to cool.

2. Measure the hot fudge sauce in a microwave-safe container and set in the microwave.

step 4

serve

1. Divide tortilla chips among 4 soup bowls. Top with the beef and bean mixture. Serve with the salad platter.

2. When ready for dessert, microwave the hot fudge sauce on High for 30 seconds. Scoop the sorbet into 4 dessert dishes. Spoon some hot fudge sauce over each serving of sorbet and sprinkle with 1 tablespoon of toasted almonds.

Tortilla, Beef, and Bean Bowl
Single serving is 1/4 of total recipe
CALORIES 456; PROTEIN 25g; CARBS 39g;
TOTAL FAT 26g; SAT FAT 3g; CHOLESTEROL 56mg;
SODIUM 808mg; FIBER 10g

beef and portobello stir-fry

vegetable lo mein

almond cookies and oranges

menu gameplan

---

shopping list

Lo mein noodles

Shredded carrots
(from the salad bar
or produce department)

Frozen baby peas

Sliced scallions
(from the salad bar)

Portobello mushroom slices
(from the produce department)

Beef strips cut for stir-fry

Hoisin sauce

Oranges

Almond cookies

from your pantry

Salt

Toasted sesame oil

Garlic

Peanut oil

serves 4

beforeyoustart

Bring the water to a boil in a large pot, covered, over high heat to cook the lo mein noodles. Chill the oranges.

step	1	cook the **vegetable lo mein**

step	2	cook the **beef and portobello stir-fry**

step	3	**serve**

 **heads**up Beef precut for stir-fry is most often from the top round, a lean cut that gets tough when overcooked. And the stir-fry strips do cook quickly, so remove them from the pan as soon as they are browned.

"Toothsome is the word that applies here. I chose portobello mushrooms because they are almost as meaty as beef."

—minutemeals' chef David

step 1

cook the **vegetable lo mein**

8 ounces lo mein noodles

1 cup shredded carrots

1 cup frozen baby peas

1 teaspoon toasted sesame oil

1/4 sliced scallions

1. Bring a large pot of water to a boil, covered, over high heat. Add salt. Stir in the noodles and cook according to the directions on the package. One minute before the noodles are done, stir in the carrots and baby peas.

2. Drain the noodles and return to the pot. Add the sesame oil and toss well to coat the noodles completely. Cover to keep warm.

step 2

cook the **beef and portobello stir-fry**

4 garlic cloves, thinly sliced

2 packages (6 ounces each) portobello mushroom slices

2 tablespoons peanut oil

1 pound beef strips cut for stir-fry

3 tablespoons hoisin sauce

1. Thinly slice the garlic cloves. Cut the portobello slices in half.

2. Heat 1 tablespoon oil in a large deep nonstick skillet over medium-high heat. Add the beef and season with salt to taste; stir-fry until no longer pink and transfer to a bowl.

3. Return the skillet to the heat. Add the remaining 1 tablespoon oil and the garlic and cook, stirring, 30 seconds. Add the sliced portobello mushrooms and stir-fry, until mushrooms are tender, 5 to 6 minutes.

4. Return the beef and any juices to the skillet. Stir the hoisin sauce and 2 tablespoons water into the skillet. Cook 1 minute, until the beef and mushrooms are well coated.

step 3

serve

1. Divide the noodles among 4 dinner plates and sprinkle with the chopped scallions.

2. Add a serving of the beef and mushrooms to each plate.

3. When ready for dessert, slice the oranges into wedges and serve with the almond cookies.

Beef and Portobello Stir-Fry
Single serving is 1/4 of total recipe
CALORIES 294; PROTEIN 26g; CARBS 9g;
TOTAL FAT 15g; SAT FAT 4g; CHOLESTEROL 64mg;
SODIUM 402mg; FIBER 1g

garlic-mustard crusted steak

bitter greens and white beans

red and yellow
cherry tomatoes

crusty sourdough bread

fresh fruit tart

menu gameplan

shopping list

Boneless beef for
London broil

Prewashed European
salad mix (escarole, endive,
and radicchio)

Cannellini beans

Red and yellow cherry
tomatoes

Crusty sourdough bread
or rolls

Fresh fruit tart

from your pantry

Salt

Freshly ground black pepper

Garlic

Plain dried bread crumbs

Dijon mustard

Olive oil

beforeyoustart

Preheat the broiler to cook the steak.

step 1 make the **garlic-mustard crusted steak**

step 2 make the **bitter greens and white beans**

step 3 **serve**

headsup

The label "London broil" on a steak says more about how you should cook the steak than about the part of the cow it's from. The term is used for flank steak, top round, and boneless top sirloin. To prepare it à la London broil, cook it just to rare, and slice it thinly at an angle, across the grain.

"After one bite of the steak, you'll lean back in your chair, close your eyes, and sigh."

—minutemeals' chef Wendy

step 1

make the **garlic-mustard crusted steak**

1 1/2 pounds boneless beef for London broil, about 1 inch thick, trimmed

2 garlic cloves

1/2 cup plain dried bread crumbs

1 tablespoon Dijon mustard

1. Preheat the broiler. Line a broiler pan with aluminum foil. Season the steak with salt and pepper to taste and place on the broiler pan rack. Broil the steak 6 inches from the heat for 10 minutes.

2. Meanwhile, mince the garlic. In a small bowl, combine the bread crumbs, mustard, and garlic until the mixture holds together.

3. Turn the steak; it will be rare. Press the bread crumb mixture onto the top of the steak and broil 5 minutes longer, until the topping is browned and the steak is medium-rare. Transfer the steak to a cutting board.

step 2

make the **bitter greens and white beans**

3 garlic cloves, lightly crushed

1 tablespoon olive oil

2 bags (7 ounces each) prewashed European salad mix (escarole, endive, and radicchio)

1 can (15 ounces) cannellini beans, rinsed and drained

1. Crush the garlic cloves with the flat side of a chef's knife and pick off the skin. Place the olive oil and the garlic cloves in a large deep skillet or Dutch oven. Cook over medium-high heat for 1 minute, stirring often, until the garlic is golden.

2. Add the greens mixture and 1/4 cup water. Toss well, then cover and cook for 2 minutes, stirring occasionally, until the greens have wilted.

3. Drain and rinse the beans. Stir the beans into the skillet. Season with salt and pepper to taste. Cover and cook about 45 seconds longer, until the beans are heated through.

step 3

serve

1. Rinse the cherry tomatoes and put them in a bowl. Put the sourdough bread on a cutting board with a serrated knife. Bring the tomatoes and bread to the table.

2. Cut the steak in thin slices across the grain and arrange down the center of a large serving platter. Surround the steak with the greens and beans. Serve.

3. When ready for dessert, slice the fresh fruit tart and serve.

Garlic-Mustard Crusted Steak
Single serving is 1/4 of total recipe

CALORIES 321; PROTEIN 36g; CARBS 11g; TOTAL FAT 14g; SAT FAT 6g; CHOLESTEROL 84mg; SODIUM 461mg; FIBER 0g

broiled strip steak
with scallions
coleslaw with apples
buttermilk biscuits with honey
carrot cake

menu gameplan

serves 4

beforeyoustart

Preheat the broiler for the steak and scallions.

step	1	make the **broiled strip steak with scallions**
step	2	warm the **buttermilk biscuits**
step	3	make the **coleslaw with apples**
step	4	**serve**

shopping list

Strip steaks

Chopped garlic in oil

Scallions

Buttermilk biscuits

Apples

Pre-shredded green cabbage or coleslaw mix

Carrot cake

from your pantry

Salt

Freshly ground black pepper

Olive oil

Honey

Mayonnaise

Cider vinegar

Sugar

luckyforyou
These days, many super-markets carry classy cuts of beef like the strip, so don't assume you need to make a special trip to the butcher to make this menu.

"When you throw a party, you should be able to enjoy it. A fine steak is special-occasion fare without fuss." —minutemeals' chef Wendy

make the **broiled strip steak with scallions**

4 strip steaks (each about 8 ounces and 3/4 inch thick)

1 tablespoon chopped garlic in oil

3 bunches scallions

1 tablespoon olive oil

1. Preheat the broiler. Line a broiler pan with aluminum foil. Place the steaks on the broiler-pan rack and rub with the chopped garlic. Season with salt and freshly ground black pepper to taste. Broil the steaks 4 inches from the heat for 10 to 12 minutes, turning once, for medium-rare. Transfer the steaks to a platter.

2. Trim the root ends and any tough outer skins from the scallions. Cut off and discard all but 3 inches of the green tops. Arrange the scallions in a jelly-roll pan. Drizzle with olive oil and season with salt and pepper.

3. Broil the scallions 4 inches from the heat for 3 minutes, turning once, until lightly browned and tender.

warm the **buttermilk biscuits**

1 package buttermilk biscuits

1/4 cup honey

In a toaster oven, warm the biscuits according to the directions on the package. Place the honey in a small bowl and set on the table.

make the **coleslaw with apples**

2 crisp apples

1 bag (1 pound) pre-shredded green cabbage or coleslaw mix

1/2 cup mayonnaise, low-fat or regular

2 tablespoons cider vinegar

1 tablespoon sugar

In a large bowl grate the apples, discarding the cores. Add the coleslaw mix, mayonnaise, vinegar, sugar, and a generous grinding of black pepper. Toss to combine and place the bowl on the table.

serve

1. Transfer the warm biscuits to a napkin-lined basket and set on the table.

2. Mound the scallions on top of the steaks and bring to the table. Serve with the slaw and biscuits.

3. When ready for dessert, slice the carrot cake and serve.

Broiled Strip Steak with Scallions
Single serving is 1/4 of total recipe

CALORIES 321; PROTEIN 38g; CARBS 6g; TOTAL FAT 16g; SAT FAT 5g; CHOLESTEROL 97mg; SODIUM 245mg; FIBER 2g

sirloin steak
with tomato vinaigrette

micro-baked potatoes
with scallion cream cheese

hearts of romaine with
blue cheese dressing

pink grapefruit sorbet with
vodka and almond cookies

shopping list

Baking potatoes

Chive and onion or vegetable
cream cheese

Boneless sirloin steak

Cherry tomatoes
(from the salad bar)

Fresh basil

Hearts of romaine

Crumbled blue cheese

Grapefruit sorbet

Vodka or Campari, if desired

Almond cookies

from your pantry

Garlic

Vinaigrette dressing,
store-bought or homemade

Salt

Freshly ground black pepper

Extra virgin olive oil

Red wine vinegar

serves 4

beforeyoustart
Preheat the broiler to cook the steak.

step 1 make the **micro-baked potatoes with scallion cream cheese**

step 2 make the **sirloin steak with tomato vinaigrette**

step 3 prepare the **hearts of romaine with blue cheese dressing**

step 4 serve

luckyforyou
The few minutes needed to make the vinaigrette and salad give the steak just the right amount of resting time. That's the interval between cooking and slicing that allows the meat's juices, which have been driven to the center of the steak by the heat, to redistribute throughout the meat.

"That's right—real meat and potatoes in 20 minutes! This menu feels old-fashioned, but fits a modern, busy schedule." —minutemeals' chef Hillary

step 1

make the **micro-baked potatoes with scallion cream cheese**

4 baking potatoes
(7 to 8 ounces each)

1 container (8 ounces)
chive and onion or vegetable
cream cheese

Pierce each potato twice with a fork. Arrange the potatoes spoke-fashion in the microwave. Microwave on High for 14 to 16 minutes.

step 2

make the **sirloin steak with tomato vinaigrette**

for the steak

1¹/₂ pounds boneless sirloin
steak, at least 1 inch thick

2 garlic cloves, minced

2 tablespoons vinaigrette
dressing

for the tomato vinaigrette

2 pints cherry tomatoes,
stemmed and halved

2 tablespoons chopped fresh
basil or 2 teaspoons dried

¹/₄ cup vinaigrette dressing

1. Make the steak: Preheat the broiler. Pierce the steak 4 to 5 times with a meat fork or the tip of a sharp knife. Mince the garlic. Spread the vinaigrette dressing, garlic, and salt and pepper to taste on both sides of the steak. Place the steak on the broiler-pan rack.

2. Broil the steak 3 to 4 inches from the heat for 5 to 7 minutes on each side for medium-rare. Transfer the steak to a cutting board and tent loosely with aluminum foil.

3. Make the vinaigrette: Stem, rinse, and halve the cherry tomatoes. Place in a medium bowl. Rinse and chop enough basil to measure 2 tablespoons, and add to the tomatoes. Stir in the vinaigrette and salt and pepper to taste and place the bowl on the table.

step 3

prepare the **hearts of romaine with blue cheese dressing**

2 hearts of romaine

2 tablespoons extra-virgin
olive oil

1 tablespoon red wine vinegar

¹/₄ cup crumbled blue cheese

Quarter each heart of romaine and lay the quarters close together on a serving platter. Drizzle first the olive oil and then the vinegar over the romaine. Season with salt to taste and a generous grinding of black pepper. Scatter the blue cheese on top. Place the salad on the table.

step 4

serve

1. Cut the steaks into thin slices across the grain and arrange on 4 dinner plates. Spoon some of the tomato vinaigrette over each serving.

2. Place a baked potato on each plate and pass the scallion cream cheese for topping.

3. When ready for dessert, serve scoops of the grapefruit sorbet, splashed with a bit of vodka or Campari, if desired, and the almond cookies.

Sirloin Steak with Tomato Vinaigrette
Single serving is ¹/₄ of total recipe

CALORIES 298; PROTEIN 39g; CARBS 1g;
TOTAL FAT 14g; SAT FAT 5g; CHOLESTEROL 115mg;
SODIUM 288mg; FIBER 0g

philly cheese steaks italiano

cucumber and radish salad

semolina-garlic toasts

chocolate chip cookie sundaes

menu gameplan

serves 4

beforeyoustart

Preheat the broiler to make the semolina-garlic toasts.

step	1	cook the **semolina-garlic toasts**
step	2	cook the **philly cheese steaks italiano**
step	3	assemble the **cucumber and radish salad**
step	4	**serve**

shopping list

Italian semolina bread

Fruity olive oil

Thin-sliced boneless sirloin steaks

Jarred sliced banana peppers or pepperoncini

Thin-sliced provolone cheese

Radishes

Vanilla ice cream

Chocolate chip cookies

from the salad bar

Red onion slices

Green or red pepper slices

Cucumber slices

from your pantry

Garlic

Salt and pepper

Cooking spray

Cider vinegar

Canola oil

Sugar

Chocolate syrup

headsup If you find the thinly-sliced beef labeled "for bracciole," you can certainly buy it for the steaks. Bracciole is generally cut from top round, which is slightly less tender than sirloin, but if you cook it briefly as the recipe directs, the steaks will be just fine.

"You can dress these down. Forget the silverware—pile everything on hero rolls. Prefer American cheese? Go for it."

—minutemeals' chef David

step 1

cook the **semolina-garlic toasts**

- 1 garlic clove, peeled and halved
- 4 large slices Italian semolina bread, halved (or 8 small slices)
- 2 teaspoons fruity olive oil

1. Preheat the broiler. Peel and halve the garlic clove.

2. Place the bread on a baking sheet and broil 3 to 5 inches from the heat, turning once, until toasted. Remove the toasts from the oven and let cool slightly.

3. Drizzle each toast with some of the olive oil and rub with the cut sides of the garlic clove.

step 2

cook the **philly cheese steaks italiano**

- 4 thin-sliced boneless sirloin steaks (5 to 6 ounces each)
- 1 cup red onion slices
- 1 cup green or red pepper slices
- 1/4 cup well-drained sliced banana peppers or pepperoncini
- 8 thin slices provolone cheese

1. Place a large heavy or cast-iron skillet over medium-high heat and heat for 1 minute. While it heats, generously season the steaks with salt and pepper to taste.

2. Add the steaks to the skillet and cook, turning once, until medium-rare, 5 to 6 minutes. Transfer steaks to a plate.

3. While the steaks cook, spray a large nonstick skillet with cooking spray and heat over medium-high heat. Add the onion, red or green peppers, and banana peppers, and sprinkle with salt and pepper. Cook the vegetables until softened, 5 to 7 minutes.

4. Push the vegetables to one side of the skillet. Add the steaks and spoon the vegetables over each steak. Top each steak with 2 slices of the provolone cheese, overlapping the slices to fit. Cover the skillet and remove from the heat. Let the steaks stand for about 1 minute, or until the cheese melts.

step 3

while the steaks cook, assemble the **cucumber and radish salad**

- 6 radishes, thinly sliced
- 4 cups cucumber slices
- 2 tablespoons cider vinegar
- 1 tablespoon canola oil
- 1 1/2 tablespoons sugar

Trim and thinly slice the radishes. Combine the radishes, cucumbers, vinegar, oil, and sugar in a bowl and toss well. Season with salt and pepper to taste.

step 4

serve

1. Divide the garlic toasts among 4 dinner plates. Add a cheese steak to each plate and serve with the salad.

2. When ready for dessert, place 2 scoops of vanilla ice cream in each of 4 sundae glasses. Crumble 2 chocolate chip cookies over each serving and drizzle with 2 tablespoons of chocolate syrup.

Philly Cheese Steaks Italiano
Single serving is 1/4 of total recipe
CALORIES 338; PROTEIN 40g; CARBS 5g;
TOTAL FAT 17g; SAT FAT 8g; CHOLESTEROL 116mg;
SODIUM 648mg; FIBER 1g

cajun pork chops
cheddar mashed potatoes
crunchy carrot salad
ripe pears and oatmeal cookies

serves 4

step 1 cook the **cajun pork chops**

step 2 heat the **cheddar mashed potatoes**

step 3 assemble the **crunchy carrot salad**

step 4 **serve**

shopping list

Boneless pork loin chops

Red onion slices
(from the salad bar)

Barbecue sauce

Scallions

Prepared mashed potatoes
(from the refrigerated section
of the produce department)

Frozen corn

Pre-grated Cheddar cheese

Shredded carrots
(from the salad bar
or produce department)

Honey-mustard
salad dressing

Dried cranberries

Chopped pecans

Ripe pears

Oatmeal cookies

from your pantry

Vegetable oil

Cajun seasoning

Salt and pepper

 Refrigerated mashed potatoes can be hot and ready to serve in less than 10 minutes. And you can dress them up with very little effort: For starters, try stirring in flavored cheese, including the soft herbed cheese spreads, horseradish, sun-dried tomatoes, or bacon bits.

"Slow-cooked ribs are a weekend treat, but I found a way to treat myself on a weeknight—without messy fingers."

—minutemeals' chef Sarah

step 1

cook the **cajun pork chops**

1 tablespoon vegetable oil

4 boneless pork loin chops, each about 3/4 inch thick (about 1 1/4 pounds in all), trimmed

2 teaspoons Cajun seasoning

1 cup red onion slices

1/2 cup barbecue sauce

1. Heat the oil in a large heavy skillet over medium-high heat. Sprinkle the pork chops on both sides with the Cajun seasoning.

2. Add the pork chops and red onion slices to the skillet. Cook until the pork chops are browned, about 6 minutes, turning once.

3. Stir in the barbecue sauce and 1/2 cup water. Cover and cook, turning the pork chops once, until no longer pink in the center but still juicy, 3 to 4 minutes longer.

4. Remove the pork chops to a plate. Let the sauce simmer, uncovered, to thicken slightly, about 1 minute. Return the chops to the skillet and remove from the heat. Partially cover to keep warm.

step 2

heat the **cheddar mashed potatoes**

2 scallions, thinly sliced

1 package (1 pound, 4 ounces) prepared mashed potatoes

1/2 cup frozen corn

1/2 cup pre-grated Cheddar cheese

1. Thinly slice the scallions. Uncover the potatoes and stir in the scallions and corn. Cover the potatoes and microwave on High, stirring occasionally until heated, 4 to 6 minutes.

2. Add the cheese and microwave until it melts, about 1 minute. Stir and cover to keep hot.

step 3

assemble the **crunchy carrot salad**

2 cups shredded carrots

3 tablespoons honey-mustard salad dressing

1/4 cup dried cranberries

1/4 cup chopped pecans

Combine the carrots, salad dressing, cranberries, and pecans in a salad bowl. Season with salt and pepper to taste and toss to coat with the dressing.

step 4

serve

1. Divide the pork chops among 4 dinner plates and spoon the sauce and onions over the chops. Serve with the mashed potatoes and the carrot salad.

2. When ready for dessert, rinse the pears and arrange them in a bowl. Serve with the oatmeal cookies.

Cajun Pork Chops
Single serving is 1/4 of total recipe
CALORIES 285; PROTEIN 33g; CARBS 7g;
TOTAL FAT 13g; SAT FAT 4g; CHOLESTEROL 92mg;
SODIUM 559mg; FIBER 1g

pork chops
with creamy dijon sauce
tiny potatoes with chives
micro-steamed broccoli and baby carrots
soft molasses cookies and crisp apples

menu
gameplan

serves 4

shopping list

Small white or red
thin-skinned potatoes

Chives or scallions

Boneless pork loin chops

Heavy cream

Broccoli florets
(from the salad bar
or produce department)

Baby carrots

Soft molasses cookies

Crisp apples

from your pantry

Salt

Butter

Freshly ground black pepper

All-purpose flour

Grainy Dijon mustard

Dried tarragon

step **1** make the **tiny potatoes with chives**

step **2** make the **pork chops with creamy dijon sauce**

step **3** prepare the **micro-steamed broccoli and baby carrots**

step **4** **serve**

headsup You can save time here by substituting good bread or rolls for the boiled potatoes. Just be sure to serve some starch for soaking up every last bit of the mustard-cream sauce.

"I always have good mustard on hand. That's what allowed me to whip up this special but impromptu dinner."

—minutemeals' chef Miriam

step 1

make the **tiny potatoes with chives**

1 pound small white or red thin-skinned potatoes

2 tablespoons snipped fresh chives or scallion greens

1 tablespoon butter

1. Rinse the potatoes and cut each in half. Place in a medium saucepan and add water to reach 1 inch. Add salt to taste, cover, and bring to a boil over high heat. Reduce the heat to medium-low, cover and simmer until potatoes are fork-tender, 12 to 14 minutes.

2. Meanwhile, finely snip enough chives or scallion greens to measure 2 tablespoons.

3. Drain the potatoes and return to the cooking pot. Add the butter and chives or scallion greens; season to taste with salt and freshly ground black pepper. Toss gently to melt the butter. Cover to keep warm.

step 2

make the **pork chops with creamy dijon sauce**

3 tablespoons all-purpose flour

4 boneless pork loin chops, each about 4 ounces and 3/4 inch thick, trimmed

2 tablespoons butter

1/2 cup heavy cream

1 tablespoon grainy Dijon mustard

1. Put the flour in a pie plate or on a sheet of waxed paper. Season the chops well with salt and pepper. Coat the chops in the flour; discard any remaining flour.

2. Melt the butter in a large heavy skillet (nonstick is fine) over medium heat. Add the chops to the pan; increase the heat to medium-high. Cook the chops, turning once, until golden brown and slightly crusty on the outside but still juicy and a little pink on the inside, 7 to 8 minutes. Transfer chops to a serving platter.

3. Add the cream and mustard to the skillet and whisk to blend well. Bring to a simmer. Reduce heat to low and simmer, stirring often, until thickened, about 2 minutes.

4. Pour any juices from the pork into the sauce and simmer 30 seconds longer. Remove from the heat. Season with salt and pepper to taste and pour over the chops.

step 3

prepare the **micro-steamed broccoli and baby carrots**

8 ounces broccoli florets

8 ounces baby carrots

1 teaspoon butter

1/2 teaspoon dried tarragon

1. Place the broccoli and carrots in a large microwave-safe dish. Sprinkle with 3 tablespoons water. Cover with a lid or vented plastic wrap.

2. Microwave on High for 6 to 8 minutes, stirring halfway through cooking, until crisp-tender. Drain. Transfer the vegetables to a serving bowl, and toss with the butter. Sprinkle with the dried tarragon, season with salt and pepper to taste, and toss again. Place the bowl on the table.

step 4

serve

1. Transfer the potatoes to a serving bowl and place the bowl on the table. Place the pork chops on the table. Serve the pork and potatoes with the broccoli and carrots.

2. When ready for dessert, serve the molasses cookies with the apples.

Pork Chops with Creamy Dijon Sauce
Single serving is 1/4 of total recipe

CALORIES 342; PROTEIN 23g; CARBS 5g; TOTAL FAT 25g; SAT FAT 13g; CHOLESTEROL 114mg; SODIUM 297mg; FIBER 1g

pork tenderloin
with caramelized onions
buttered asparagus with parmesan cheese
poppy seed foccacia
angel food cake with blueberry topping

shopping list

Pork tenderloin

Red onions

Asparagus

Blueberry or your favorite jam

Lemon (for juice)

Angel food cake

Poppy seed or plain focaccia

from your pantry

Salt

Freshly ground black pepper

Butter

White balsamic vinegar

Dried thyme

Grated Parmesan cheese

Ground allspice

serves 4

beforeyoustart
Preheat the broiler to cook the pork tenderloin.

step 1 cook the **pork tenderloin with caramelized onions**

step 2 make the **buttered asparagus with parmesan cheese**

step 3 prepare the **angel food cake with blueberry topping**

step 4 serve

luckyforyou
A pork tenderloin can weigh from 1 to 2 pounds and is often sold two to a pack—which gives you the perfect excuse to double the recipe. It won't take any longer to roast two tenderloins (use red onion slices from the salad bar to save slicing time), and the leftover pork makes a knockout sandwich.

"This is straightforward food. I wanted to bring out the true flavors of the ingredients, and classic techniques do that."

—minutemeals' chef Paul

step 1

cook the **pork tenderloin with caramelized onions**

1 pork tenderloin, about 1¼ pounds

2 tablespoons butter

2 large red onions

2 tablespoons white balsamic vinegar

1 teaspoon dried thyme, crumbled

1. Preheat the broiler. Line the broiler pan or a roasting pan with heavy-duty aluminum foil. Place the pork tenderloin in the prepared pan. Season with salt and freshly ground black pepper to taste. Broil 4 inches from the heat for 12 to 15 minutes, turning occasionally, until browned and just a little pink in the center; when done, the internal temperature should register 155°F on a meat thermometer. Transfer the pork to a cutting board.

2. Meanwhile, melt the butter in a large nonstick skillet over medium-high heat. Halve and thinly slice the onions, adding them to the skillet as you slice. Cook, uncovered, for 8 minutes, stirring occasionally, until the onions are softened and beginning to caramelize. Stir in the vinegar, ⅓ cup water, and thyme, and season with salt and pepper. Cook, uncovered, for 2 minutes longer, or until the liquid is almost evaporated and the onions are very tender.

step 2

while the pork cooks, make the **buttered asparagus with parmesan cheese**

1 pound fresh asparagus, trimmed

3 tablespoons grated Parmesan cheese

1 tablespoon butter

Place the asparagus in a shallow microwave-safe dish. Add 2 tablespoons water. Cover with a lid or vented plastic wrap and microwave on High for 4 to 5 minutes or until just fork-tender. Drain well. Add the Parmesan cheese and butter and toss. Season with salt and freshly ground black pepper to taste.

step 3

prepare the **angel food cake with blueberry topping**

½ cup blueberry or your favorite jam

1 tablespoon lemon juice

⅛ teaspoon ground allspice

Angel food cake

Measure jam in a microwave-safe measuring cup. Stir in the lemon juice and allspice.

step 4

serve

1. Slice the foccacia into squares and arrange in a napkin-lined basket.

2. Spoon the onion mixture onto one end of a large serving platter. Slice the pork and arrange on the other end. Serve with the bread and the asparagus.

3. When ready for dessert, microwave the blueberry sauce on High for 30 seconds. Slice the cake and place a piece on each of 4 dessert plates. Stir the sauce and spoon over the cake slices; serve.

Pork Tenderloin with Caramelized Onions
Single serving is ¼ of total recipe

CALORIES 253; PROTEIN 31g; CARBS 6g; TOTAL FAT 11g; SAT FAT 5g; CHOLESTEROL 100mg; SODIUM 267mg; FIBER 1g

pork and black bean burritos

chopped salad with guacamole dressing

key lime pie

menu gameplan

shopping list

Flour tortillas
(10-inch diameter)

Pork tenderloin

Salsa verde

Black beans

Pre-grated Monterey Jack cheese

Guacamole

Red wine vinegar and oil salad dressing

Cucumber slices
(from the salad bar)

Red onion slices
(from the salad bar)

Prewashed chopped iceberg lettuce

Key lime pie

from your pantry

Olive oil cooking spray

Salt and pepper

serves 4

beforeyoustart

Preheat the broiler to cook the pork and warm the tortillas.

step 1 make the **pork and black bean burritos**

step 2 assemble the **chopped salad with guacamole dressing**

step 3 **serve**

headsup

Salsa verde, a piquant mix of raw chopped tomatillos, chiles, and cilantro, hasn't gained quite the popularity of red salsa, but you should be able to find it at your supermarket. Check both the Mexican/Spanish section, and the chip shelves, where red salsas are found.

"These burritos are big guys. If you are feeding wee diners, halve the filled burritos or use smaller tortillas."

—minutemeals' chef Lisa

step 1
make the **pork and black bean burritos**

4 flour tortillas (10-inch diameter)

1 pork tenderloin (about 1¼ pounds), trimmed

1¼ cups salsa verde

1 can (15 ounces) black beans, drained and rinsed

1½ cups pre-grated Monterey Jack cheese

1. Preheat the broiler. Place 1 oven rack 6 inches from the heat, and another rack toward the bottom of the oven. Wrap the tortillas in aluminum foil and put them on the lower rack while the oven heats.

2. Line a jelly-roll pan or the bottom of the broiler pan with aluminum foil and spray the foil with olive oil cooking spray. Halve the pork tenderloin lengthwise and place the halves on the prepared pan. Season with salt and pepper to taste.

3. Spoon 3 to 4 tablespoons of the salsa over each half. Broil the pork 3 to 4 minutes, until it is no longer pink on the outside and beginning to feel firm. Turn each half, spread another 3 tablespoons of salsa over each, and broil 3 to 4 minutes longer, or until the pork is a little pink inside and still juicy. Transfer pork to a cutting board and remove the tortillas from the oven.

4. Meanwhile, drain and rinse the beans. In a large nonstick skillet, stir together the beans and the remaining salsa. Cover and bring to a boil over medium heat.

5. Cut the pork crosswise into thin slices and add them and any pork juices to the beans. Warm through for 1 minute.

step 2
assemble the **chopped salad with guacamole dressing**

½ cup prepared guacamole

¼ cup red wine vinegar and oil salad dressing

2 cups cucumber slices

1 cup red onion slices

1 package (8 ounces) prewashed chopped iceberg lettuce

1. In a salad bowl whisk together the guacamole and salad dressing.

2. Coarsely chop the cucumber and red onion slices. Add the lettuce and chopped cucumber and red onion slices to the dressing. Toss, season with salt and pepper to taste, and toss again. Place the bowl on the table.

step 3
serve

1. Lay a warm tortilla on each of 4 plates. Divide the filling among the tortillas, sprinkle each with some of the cheese, and roll up. Serve with the salad.

2. When ready for dessert, slice the Key lime pie and serve.

Pork and Black Bean Burritos
Single serving is ¼ of total recipe

CALORIES 652; PROTEIN 50g; CARBS 55g; TOTAL FAT 24g; SAT FAT 11g; CHOLESTEROL 122mg; SODIUM 1148mg; FIBER 6g

clt pizza
(pizza with cappicola, lettuce, and tomato)
artichoke and olive salad
black and white ice cream sandwiches

menu
gameplan

serves 4

shopping list

Plum tomatoes

Prebaked pizza crust

Marinated mozzarella balls

Thinly sliced hot cappicola

Prewashed spring salad mix

Jarred roasted red peppers

Jarred marinated artichoke hearts

Marinated pitted olives

Zesty Italian salad dressing

Chocolate sorbet

Sugar cookies

Chopped toffee bits

from your pantry

Freshly ground black pepper

beforeyoustart
Adjust an oven rack to the lower third of the oven and preheat the oven to 450°F to cook the pizza.

step 1 make the **clt pizza**

step 2 make the **artichoke and olive salad**

step 3 assemble the **black and white ice cream sandwiches**

step 4 **serve**

luckyforyou You can purchase most of the ingredients for this menu right at your supermarket deli section. You'll find the cappicola there, along with the mozzarella balls and most of the salad ingredients (which are also available jarred). The deli should carry hot cappicola, which is coated with a spicy red pepper mixture. Ask the deli worker to slice the cappicola very thin.

"You could always order salad pizza for delivery, but you'll never get one so fresh from a box."

—minutemeals' chef Sarah

step 1

make the **clt pizza**

3 plum tomatoes, sliced

1 (10 ounce) prebaked pizza crust

12 small (1-inch) marinated fresh mozzarella balls, with 2 teaspoons of the marinade set aside

3 ounces thinly sliced hot cappicola

1/2 bag (5 ounces) prewashed spring salad mix

1. Adjust an oven rack to the lower third of the oven. Preheat the oven to 450°F. Slice the plum tomatoes.

2. Place the pizza crust on a baking sheet. Arrange the tomato slices and mozzarella balls on the crust. Arrange the cappicola on top.

3. Bake the pizza 10 to 12 minutes, or until the cheese is melted.

4. Let the pizza stand 5 minutes before serving. In a medium bowl, toss the salad mix and the 2 teaspoons reserved marinade from the mozzarella balls and toss.

step 2

make the **artichoke and olive salad**

1 jar (7 ounces) roasted red peppers, drained

1 jar (7 ounces) marinated artichoke hearts, drained

1/3 cup pitted marinated olives

1 tablespoon zesty Italian salad dressing

1. Drain the peppers and rinse. Cut into wide strips. Drain the artichokes and cut each in half.

2. Place the peppers, artichokes, and olives on a serving plate. Drizzle with the salad dressing and grind a generous amount of fresh black pepper over the top.

step 3

assemble the **black and white ice cream sandwiches**

1 pint chocolate ice cream or sorbet

8 large sugar cookies

1/4 cup chopped toffee bits

1. Peel the carton from the ice cream. Cut the ice cream into 4 slices.

2. Sandwich the ice cream slices between the sugar cookies. Roll the edges in the toffee bits to coat. Place the sandwiches on a baking sheet and freeze until serving.

step 4

serve

1. Top the warm pizza with the salad mix, and slice with a pizza wheel. Serve wedges of the pizza with salad.

2. When ready for dessert, serve the ice cream sandwiches.

CLT Pizza
Single serving is 1/4 of total recipe
CALORIES 409; PROTEIN 18g; CARBS 35g;
TOTAL FAT 22g; SAT FAT 9g; CHOLESTEROL 36mg;
SODIUM 689mg; FIBER 3g

savory lamb chops dijon

spanish rice
honey-glazed carrots
green and red grapes with butter cookies

menu gameplan

serves 4

beforeyoustart

Preheat the broiler to cook the lamb chops. Rinse and chill the grapes.

step 1 cook the **savory lamb chops dijon**

step 2 cook the **spanish rice**

step 3 cook the **honey-glazed carrots**

step 4 serve

shopping list

Shoulder lamb chops

Lemon (for juice)

Spanish rice and sauce mix

Baby carrots

Green and red grapes (from the salad bar)

Butter cookies

from your pantry

Nonstick cooking spray

Garlic

Dijon mustard

Dried thyme

Salt

Freshly ground black pepper

Butter

Honey

Ground cinnamon

heads up

Quick-cooking mixes for rice, potato, and pasta side dishes give you a wide variety of options for filling out simple meat and poultry menus. But if the mix you choose contains an abundance of sodium—and many contain as much as 25% of the recommended daily allowance—remember to go easy on the salt in the rest of the meal.

"Shoulder chops are larger than expensive rib and loin chops, so you get more surface area for smearing on seasonings."

—minutemeals' chef Ruth

step 1

cook the **savory lamb chops dijon**

4 shoulder lamb chops (6 to 8 ounces each), trimmed

2 garlic cloves

2 teaspoons lemon juice

2 tablespoons Dijon mustard

1/4 teaspoon dried thyme

1. Preheat the broiler. Line a broiler pan with aluminum foil and spray broiler pan rack with nonstick cooking spray. Trim the fat from chops and place on the prepared pan.

2. Mince the garlic. Squeeze enough lemon juice to measure 2 teaspoons. In a small bowl stir together the garlic, lemon juice, mustard, and thyme. Add salt and freshly ground black pepper to taste and mix well. Spread half of the mixture over the chops.

3. Broil the chops 6 inches from the heat for 5 minutes. Turn and spread with remaining mustard mixture. Broil 4 to 6 minutes longer for medium.

step 2

cook the **spanish rice**

1 package (about 6 ounces) Spanish rice and sauce mix

Butter or oil, if desired

Cook the Spanish rice mix with the amount of water and for the time directed on the package, adding butter or oil as directed, if desired. Remove from the heat, and keep warm until serving time.

step 3

cook the **honey-glazed carrots**

1 bag (16 ounces) baby carrots

2 tablespoons honey

1 tablespoon butter

1/4 teaspoon cinnamon

1. Place the carrots in a medium saucepan with water to cover. Cover and bring to a boil over high heat. Reduce the heat slightly and boil for 8 minutes, or until just tender. Drain.

2. Return the carrots to the saucepan and add the honey, butter, and cinnamon. Cook over low heat, tossing gently, for 2 minutes. Season to taste with salt and pepper. Transfer to a serving dish and place on the table.

step 4

serve

1. Place a lamb chop on each of 4 dinner plates. Add a serving of Spanish rice and glazed carrots to each plate.

2. When ready for dessert, place the grapes in a bowl and serve with the butter cookies.

Savory Lamb Chops Dijon
Single serving is 1/4 of total recipe

CALORIES 188; PROTEIN 24g; CARBS 4g; TOTAL FAT 8g; SAT FAT 3g; CHOLESTEROL 75mg; SODIUM 404mg; FIBER 2g

lamb chops
with olive relish

brown rice with almonds

mixed spring greens with greek salad dressing

warm glazed pineapple with vanilla ice cream

shopping list

Shoulder lamb chops

Pitted kalamata or other flavorful black olives

Plum tomatoes or tomatoes-on-the-vine

Red onion slices (from the salad bar)

Slivered almonds

Prewashed spring greens mix

Greek or Italian salad dressing

Pineapple slices (fresh from the produce department, or juice-packed canned)

Vanilla ice cream or pineapple sorbet

from your pantry

Cooking spray

Dried oregano

Salt and pepper

Olive oil

Instant brown rice

Dark rum (optional)

Brown sugar

serves 4

beforeyoustart

Preheat the broiler. Bring the water to a boil in a medium saucepan, covered, over high heat.

step	1	make the **lamb chops with olive relish**
step	2	cook the **brown rice with almonds**
step	3	prepare the **mixed spring greens with greek salad dressing**
step	4	prepare the **warm glazed pineapple**
step	5	**serve**

 Many people are wary of rare meat, especially lamb. For those folks, shoulder lamb chops are a winner: Cheaper than rib or loin lamb chops, they are also tastier when cooked to medium. Even so, they need only 10 minutes to cook through.

"The only way I'd improve on this menu is by adding a bottle of red wine. Nothing fancy—think Greek taverna."

—minutemeals' chef Ruth

step 1

make the **lamb chops with olive relish**

4 shoulder lamb chops, 3/4 inch thick (about 1 1/2 pounds)

1 teaspoon dried oregano

1 cup pitted kalamata or other flavorful black olives, drained

3 ripe plum tomatoes (or 2 medium tomatoes-on-the-vine)

1/2 cup red onion slices

1. Preheat the broiler. Line a broiler pan with foil and spray broiler-pan rack with cooking spray. Trim the fat from chops, sprinkle on both sides with oregano, and salt and pepper to taste, and place on the prepared pan. Broil the chops 6 inches from the heat for about 5 minutes; turn, and broil 4 to 6 minutes longer for medium. Leave the broiler on to make the dessert.

2. Meanwhile, coarsely chop the olives and place in a small bowl. Coarsely chop the tomatoes and onion slices and add to the olives. Season with salt and pepper to taste.

step 2

cook the **brown rice with almonds**

1 tablespoon olive oil

3 tablespoons slivered almonds

2 cups instant brown rice

1. In a medium saucepan heat olive oil over medium heat. Add the almonds and cook, stirring frequently, for 2 minutes.

2. Add 1 3/4 cups water, cover, and bring to a boil. Stir in the rice. Return to a boil, reduce the heat to low, cover, and simmer 5 minutes. Remove pan from heat and stir; cover, place on the table, and let stand 5 minutes.

step 3

prepare the **mixed spring greens with greek salad dressing**

1 bag (5 ounces) prewashed spring greens mix

1/4 cup Greek or Italian salad dressing

Place greens in a salad bowl. Add dressing to taste and toss to coat all leaves. Place the salad on the table.

step 4

prepare the **warm glazed pineapple**

4 fresh or canned juice-packed pineapple slices

4 teaspoons dark rum (optional)

4 teaspoons brown sugar

Vanilla ice cream or pineapple sorbet

Line a jelly-roll pan with aluminum foil. Place pineapple slices in a single layer on the prepared pan. Drizzle with the rum, if using, and sprinkle each with 1 teaspoon of brown sugar.

step 5

serve

1. Season the rice with salt and pepper to taste and fluff with a fork.

2. Place 1 lamb chop on each of 4 dinner plates. Spoon some of the olive relish over each chop. Serve the chops with the rice and salad.

3. When ready for dessert, broil the pineapple 6 inches from the heat for 2 to 3 minutes or until the brown sugar is melted and bubbling. Place a ring of pineapple in the 4 small serving bowls, and top with a scoop of ice cream or sorbet. Drizzle any pan juices over the ice cream.

Lamb Chops with Olive Relish
Single serving is 1/4 of total recipe

CALORIES 275; PROTEIN 24g; CARBS 7g; TOTAL FAT 17g; SAT FAT 4g; CHOLESTEROL 75mg; SODIUM 767mg; FIBER 1g

lamb burgers
with red onion and mustard relish

cucumber and feta salad

garlic sourdough toasts

yogurt with honey, apricots, and pistachios

menu
gameplan

serves 4

beforeyoustart
Preheat the oven to 450°F to make the garlic toasts.

step 1 cook the **lamb burgers with red onion and mustard relish**

step 2 assemble the **cucumber and feta salad**

step 3 heat the **garlic sourdough toasts**

step 4 prepare the **yogurt with honey, apricots, and pistachios**

step 5 serve

shopping list

Lean ground lamb

Chopped walnuts

Red onion slices (from the salad bar)

Kirby cucumbers

Crumbled feta cheese

Sourdough bread

Plain low-fat yogurt

Dried apricots

Shelled unsalted pistachios

from your pantry

Garlic

Salt

Freshly ground black pepper

Grainy mustard

Extra virgin olive oil

Red wine vinegar

Dried oregano

Honey

heads**up**
Shaping ground meat into patties or balls can be a sticky business. If you wet your palms with cool water the meat won't stick. It's a good trick whenever you are working with tacky mixtures—try it next time you are forming cookie dough into balls.

"Mustard is a classic coating for rack of lamb, so it was a natural to pair with the lamb burgers."

—minutemeals' chef Sarah

step 1

cook the **lamb burgers with red onion and mustard relish**

1 1/2 pounds lean ground lamb

1/3 cup chopped walnuts

1 large garlic clove, crushed through a press

1 1/2 cups red onion slices

3 tablespoons grainy mustard

1. Place a large cast-iron or other heavy skillet over medium-high heat.

2. Crumble the lamb into a large bowl. Add the walnuts. Crush the garlic through a press and add to the lamb. Season with 1/2 teaspoon each salt and freshly ground black pepper. Gently work the nuts and seasonings into the meat. Shape into 4 burgers.

3. Add the burgers to the skillet and cook 14 minutes, turning once, for medium. Stack the red onion slices and quarter.

4. Transfer the burgers to a serving platter and cover loosely with foil to keep warm. Pour off any fat from the skillet and wipe with paper towels. Add the onion to the skillet and cook over medium heat for 3 minutes, or until softened. Stir in the mustard and spoon the relish over the burgers.

step 2

assemble the **cucumber and feta salad**

4 kirby cucumbers, thinly sliced

1 tablespoon extra virgin olive oil

1 tablespoon red wine vinegar

1/4 teaspoon dried oregano

1/2 cup crumbled feta cheese

1. Thinly slice the cucumbers. Place the cucumbers in a bowl and toss with the olive oil, vinegar, and oregano.

2. Turn the cucumbers onto a serving platter. Season with 1/4 teaspoon each salt and freshly ground black pepper, and scatter the feta cheese over the top. Set the platter on the table.

step 3

heat the **garlic sourdough toasts**

4 thick slices sourdough bread

1 garlic clove, halved

2 tablespoons extra virgin olive oil

1. Preheat the oven to 450°F. Place the bread slices on a baking sheet. Cut the garlic clove in half.

2. Bake the bread for 4 to 5 minutes, until lightly toasted. Rub one side of each slice with the garlic clove and drizzle with some of the olive oil.

step 4

prepare the **yogurt with honey, apricots, and pistachios**

2 cups plain low-fat yogurt

6 dried apricots, coarsely chopped

2 tablespoons shelled unsalted pistachios, coarsely chopped

3 tablespoons honey

1. Divide the yogurt among 4 dessert dishes and refrigerate.

2. Coarsely chop the apricots and pistachios.

step 5

serve

1. Place a garlic toast on each of 4 dinner plates. Set a lamb burger with onion relish on top of each toast. Serve the burgers with the cucumber salad.

2. When ready for dessert, sprinkle the yogurts with some of the apricots and pistachios and drizzle with honey.

Lamb Burgers with Red Onion and Mustard Relish
Single serving is 1/4 of total recipe
CALORIES 379; PROTEIN 45g; CARBS 6g; TOTAL FAT 18g; SAT FAT 5g; CHOLESTEROL 138mg; SODIUM 652mg; FIBER 2g

minute
5-ingredient

fish and seafood menus

meals

main dishes

colorful catfish strata

romaine and cucumber
tomato salad

parker house or sourdough
dinner rolls

lemon pound cake
with lemon sherbet

menu
gameplan

serves 4

step **1** cook the **colorful catfish strata**

step **2** assemble the **romaine and cucumber tomato salad**

step **3** **serve**

shopping list

Jarred roasted red peppers

Catfish fillets

Shredded carrots
(from the salad bar
or produce department)

Scallions

Prewashed romaine
salad mix

Cucumber slices
(from the salad bar)

Spring onion salad dressing

Parker house or sourdough
dinner rolls

Lemon pound cake

Lemon sherbet

from your pantry

Tabasco sauce

Salt and pepper

luckyforyou Catfish has a mild flavor—
milder than it used to be,
now that most catfish is farm-raised instead of wild—and
a firm texture that makes it an inexpensive substitute for
pricier fish like pompano, Dover sole, and John Dory.

"The microwave does spectacular things to fish: first among them, cooking it evenly so it's moist and tender throughout." —minutemeals' chef Ruth

step 1

cook the **colorful catfish strata**

1 jar (12 ounces) roasted red peppers, drained

1/4 teaspoon Tabasco sauce or to taste

4 catfish fillets (about 1 1/4 pounds)

2 cups shredded carrots (half of a 10-ounce bag)

4 scallions

1. Place the red peppers in a blender or food processor. Pulse for about 30 seconds or until peppers are roughly puréed. Season with Tabasco sauce.

2. Spread the pepper purée evenly in the bottom of a rectangular or round microwave-safe dish about 2 inches deep and large enough to hold the fillets without overlapping. Arrange the fillets over pepper purée. Season fish generously with salt and pepper.

3. Scatter the shredded carrots over fish. Thinly slice the white and most of the green part of the scallions and scatter over carrots. Cover dish tightly with microwave-safe plastic wrap or a lid. Microwave on High for 5 minutes. Rotate dish a half-turn. Microwave an additional 5 to 7 minutes on Medium, or until fish is steaming hot and the thinner ends flake with a fork. Let dish stand, covered, for 2 minutes.

step 2

assemble the **romaine and cucumber tomato salad**

1 package (10 ounces) prewashed romaine salad mix

2 cups cucumber slices

1/4 cup spring onion salad dressing

1. Place the romaine and cucumber slices in a salad bowl.

2. Add the salad dressing and salt and pepper to taste and toss. Place the bowl on the table.

step 3

serve

1. Place the rolls in a napkin-lined basket.

2. To serve the catfish, using a broad spatula, separate and lift fillets and their carrot and scallion topping onto 4 dinner plates. Spoon some red pepper purée next to each fillet. Serve with the salad.

3. When ready for dessert, slice the lemon pound cake and serve with scoops of lemon sherbet.

Colorful Catfish Strata
Single serving is 1/4 of total recipe

CALORIES 237; PROTEIN 22g; CARBS 15g; TOTAL FAT 10g; SAT FAT 2g; CHOLESTEROL 63mg; SODIUM 363mg; FIBER 3g

cod provençal

peas and onions
with dill and lemon

crusty baguette with butter

strawberry ice cream
with strawberry sauce

menu
gameplan

shopping list

Cod, haddock, or tilefish
fillets

Plum tomatoes

Pitted kalamata olives

Frozen baby peas and
pearl onions

Fresh dill

Lemon (for juice)

Strawberry ice cream

Frozen strawberries in syrup

Aerosol whipped cream

Chopped hazelnuts
or slivered almonds

Crusty baguette

from your pantry

Olive oil

Dried Italian herb seasoning

Salt and pepper

Butter

serves 4

beforeyoustart

Preheat the oven to 450°F to bake
the fish.

| step | 1 | cook the **cod provençal** |

| step | 2 | make the **peas and onions with dill and lemon** |

| step | 3 | prepare the **strawberry ice cream with strawberry sauce** |

| step | 4 | **serve** |

heads**up**

To ensure that the fish cooks
evenly, we call for equal-weight,
individual pieces here. That said, the dish will look lovely if
you bake two 12-ounce fillets in an oval gratin dish. If you
do, it's likely that larger fillets will have tail ends that are
noticeably thinner than the head ends. To keep the thinner
ends from cooking too quickly and drying out, fold and
tuck them underneath to make fillets of even thickness.

"If a meal can be rustic and refined, this one is. And simplicity itself—that's the glory of country French cooking."

—minutemeals' chef Paul

step 1

cook the **cod provençal**

4 cod, haddock, or tilefish fillets (6 ounces each)

1 1/2 tablespoons olive oil

3/4 teaspoon dried Italian herb seasoning

4 plum tomatoes, sliced

1/4 cup (about 1 ounce) pitted kalamata olives

1. Preheat the oven to 450°F. Arrange the cod fillets almost close together in a baking dish just large enough to hold them. Drizzle the oil over the fish and crumble the Italian seasoning on top. Slice the tomatoes and overlap some of the slices on top of each fillet. Scatter the remaining slices around the fish and season with salt and pepper to taste.

2. Bake for 10 to 12 minutes or until the fish is opaque in the center, and just barely flakes when tested with a fork. While the fish bakes, coarsely chop the olives. Remove the fish from the oven and scatter the olives on top.

step 2

while the cod cooks, make the **peas and onions with dill and lemon**

1 package (16 ounces) frozen baby peas and pearl onions

1 teaspoon snipped fresh dill

2 teaspoons fresh lemon juice (1/2 lemon)

1 tablespoon butter

1. Bring 1/3 cup water to a boil in a medium saucepan, covered, over high heat. Add the peas and onions, reduce the heat, cover, and simmer 5 to 6 minutes, until vegetables are tender.

2. Snip enough dill to measure 1 teaspoon. Squeeze 2 teaspoons lemon juice. Drain the peas and onions, return to the saucepan, and stir in the butter, snipped dill, lemon juice, and salt and pepper to taste.

step 3

prepare the **strawberry ice cream with strawberry sauce**

1 pint strawberry ice cream

1 container (16 ounces) frozen strawberries in syrup

Aerosol whipped cream

1/4 cup chopped hazelnuts or slivered almonds

Thaw the strawberries in the microwave as directed on the container.

step 4

serve

1. Place the bread and a serrated knife on a cutting board. Bring it to the table with butter.

2. Use a spatula to transfer the fish fillets to dinner plates. Spoon any tomatoes and juices in the baking dish over the fish, dividing evenly. Place a serving of peas on each plate.

3. When ready for dessert, scoop the ice cream into 4 dishes. Top each with 1/4 cup of the strawberries and their liquid. Top with whipped cream and hazelnuts or almonds.

Cod Provençal
Single serving is 1/4 of total recipe
CALORIES 170; PROTEIN 19g; CARBS 4g;
TOTAL FAT 8g; SAT FAT 1g; CHOLESTEROL 45mg;
SODIUM 367mg; FIBER 1g

baked haddock
with savory bacon crust

artichoke hearts provençal

romaine lettuce and olive salad with caesar dressing

crusty whole-grain rolls

grapes and fruit-filled cookies

menu
gameplan

shopping list

Croutons, plain or garlic-flavored

Precooked bacon

Haddock fillets

Frozen artichoke hearts

Prewashed romaine salad mix

Pitted black olives (from the salad bar or deli section)

Caesar salad dressing

Crusty whole-grain rolls

Grapes (from the salad bar)

Fruit-filled butter cookies

from your pantry

Cooking spray

Pepper

Shredded Parmesan cheese

Mayonnaise

Olive oil

Dried oregano

Crushed red pepper flakes

Salt

serves 4

beforeyoustart

Preheat the oven to 400°F to bake the fish. Rinse and chill the grapes.

step **1** cook the **baked haddock with savory bacon crust**

step **2** cook the **artichoke hearts provençal**

step **3** assemble the **salad**

step **4** **serve**

lucky**for**you

Many types of fish work well here, so feel free to shop around for the freshest, least expensive fish available. You'll need to adjust the baking time depending on the thickness of the fillets—the general rule for cooking fish, called the Canadian rule, is to allow 10 minutes per inch.

"Buzzing salad croutons in the blender makes a crumb topping that browns better and bakes up crunchier than packaged bread crumbs."

—minutemeals' chef Ruth

step 1
cook the **baked haddock with savory bacon crust**

1 cup (about) croutons, plain or garlic-flavored

2 slices precooked bacon

3 tablespoons shredded Parmesan cheese

4 haddock fillets (about 6 ounces each)

1/4 cup mayonnaise

1. Preheat the oven to 400°F. Line a baking sheet with aluminum foil and spray foil with cooking spray.

2. Pulse 1 cup croutons in a blender or food processor to rough-textured crumbs. (Or place croutons in a plastic bag and crush with a mallet or rolling pin.) Place crumbs in a small bowl. Snip the bacon into bits. Add the bacon and the cheese to the crumbs.

3. Place the fish fillets skin side down on the prepared baking sheet and season with pepper to taste. With a small spatula spread mayonnaise evenly over the fillets. Sprinkle each fillet with a thick coating of the crumb mixture, then press gently to make the crumbs adhere to the mayonnaise.

4. Bake the fish until cooked through (fish will flake with a fork but will still be moist) and the crumb mixture is crispy and lightly browned, 10 to 12 minutes, depending on the thickness of the fillets.

step 2
cook the **artichoke hearts provençal**

1 package (9 ounces) frozen artichoke hearts

1 tablespoon olive oil

1/4 teaspoon dried oregano

1/4 teaspoon crushed red pepper flakes (or to taste)

1. Cook the artichoke hearts as directed on the package; drain and return to pan.

2. Add the oil, oregano, crushed red pepper, and salt to taste. Heat gently about 1 minute, tossing lightly. Remove from the heat, and cover to keep warm.

step 3
assemble the **romaine lettuce and olive salad with caesar dressing**

1 bag (10 ounces) prewashed romaine salad mix

4 ounces small whole pitted black olives

1/4 cup Caesar salad dressing

Place the romaine in salad bowl. Drain the olives and scatter on top. Toss with the Caesar dressing and season with salt and pepper to taste. Toss again and place the bowl on the table.

step 4
serve

1. Place the rolls in a napkin-lined basket. Divide the baked fish fillets among 4 dinner plates. Add a portion of artichokes to each plate, and serve with the salad.

2. When ready for dessert, serve the grapes with the fruit-filled cookies.

Baked Haddock with Savory Bacon Crust
Single serving is 1/4 of total recipe

CALORIES 330; PROTEIN 40g; CARBS 6g;
TOTAL FAT 15g; SAT FAT 3g; CHOLESTEROL 124mg;
SODIUM 392mg; FIBER 0g

haddock poached in curry broth

rice with peas and carrots
sesame spinach salad
pineapple chunks

menu gameplan

shopping list

Bottled clam juice
Curry paste or curry powder
Haddock, halibut, or cod fillets
Fresh cilantro
Frozen peas and carrots
Prewashed baby spinach
Pineapple chunks

from your pantry

Garlic
Salt and pepper
Instant rice
Olive oil
Rice wine vinegar
Sesame seeds
Sugar

serves 4

beforeyoustart

Bring the water to a boil in a medium saucepan, covered. Chill the pineapple chunks.

| step | 1 | make the **haddock poached in curry broth** |

| step | 2 | prepare the **rice with peas and carrots** |

| step | 3 | prepare the **sesame spinach salad** |

| step | 4 | **serve** |

heads**up**

Haddock, halibut, and cod all have firm flesh and mild flavor, so they can be used interchangeably here. Or take the dish in an entirely different direction by substituting shrimp or sea scallops for the fish. If you do, be sure to reduce the poaching time by a minute or two to avoid overcooking the shellfish.

"I like to serve this dish to adult dinner guests—the presentation and exotic flavors say swank restaurant all around."

—minutemeals' chef Hillary

step 1
make the **haddock poached in curry broth**

  4 cups bottled clam juice

  3 large garlic cloves, crushed with a garlic press

  1 to 2 teaspoons curry paste or curry powder

  4 haddock, halibut, or cod fillets (6 ounces each)

  1/4 cup chopped fresh cilantro

1. In a large, deep skillet over high heat, stir together the juice, water, garlic, curry paste, salt, and pepper. Cover and bring to a boil over high heat.

2. Reduce the heat to low so that the broth is simmering and add the fish. Cover and simmer 5 to 7 minutes or until the fish is just opaque in the thickest part. Chop enough cilantro to measure 1/4 cup and stir it into the broth.

step 2
prepare the **rice with peas and carrots**

  2 cups instant rice

  1 cup frozen peas and carrots

Bring 2 cups water to a boil in a medium saucepan, covered, over high heat. Stir in the rice and the vegetables, cover, and remove from the heat. Let stand 5 minutes. Add salt and pepper to taste.

step 3
prepare the **sesame spinach salad**

  2 tablespoons olive oil

  1 tablespoon rice wine vinegar

  1 tablespoon sesame seeds

  1 1/2 teaspoons sugar

  1 bag (6 ounces) prewashed baby spinach

In a salad bowl, with a fork, whisk the olive oil, rice wine vinegar, sesame seeds, and sugar. Season with salt and pepper. Add the spinach and toss. Divide the salad among 4 salad plates and place the plates on the table.

step 4
serve

1. Fluff the rice and vegetables with a fork and season with salt and pepper. Place a fillet in each of 4 large, shallow bowls. Spoon some rice next to each fillet, and ladle some of the broth over the fish and rice. Serve with the salads.

2. Serve the chilled pineapple chunks for dessert.

Haddock Poached in Curry Broth
Single serving is 1/4 of total recipe
CALORIES 169; PROTEIN 36g; CARBS 1g; TOTAL FAT 1g; SAT FAT 0g; CHOLESTEROL 108mg; SODIUM 1411mg; FIBER 0g

soy-poached haddock

watercress rice

steamed broccoli
with sesame seeds

fortune cookies
and clementines

menu
gameplan

serves 4

beforeyoustart

Set up steamer for the broccoli and place it over simmering water.

shopping list

Watercress

Jasmine rice

Gingerroot

Mirin (sweet rice wine)

Haddock fillets

Broccoli florets
(from the salad bar
or produce department)

Clementines or
orange wedges

Fortune cookies

from your pantry

Salt

Reduced-sodium soy sauce

Brown sugar

Sesame seeds

step **1** cook the **watercress rice**

step **2** cook the **soy-poached haddock**

step **3** make the **steamed broccoli with sesame seeds**

step **4** **serve**

 Poaching is a "moist-heat" cooking method in which the heat from barely simmering liquid gently cooks the food being poached. Fish fillets benefit mightily from the method, emerging from the poaching broth tender, moist, and evenly cooked. Take care that the poaching liquid does not return to the boil once you add the fillets—if it does, the fish will shrink and toughen.

"I surprised myself with this menu—other than the fish, it contains no fat, and you don't miss it."

—minutemeals' chef Lisa

step 1

cook the **watercress rice**

2 cups coarsely chopped watercress

1 cup Jasmine rice

1. Coarsely chop the watercress and put it in a 2-quart, microwave-safe bowl.

2. Stir in the rice, 2 cups water, and ¹/₂ teaspoon salt. Cover with a lid or vented plastic wrap and microwave on High for 17 to 19 minutes, or until the rice is tender and the liquid has been absorbed.

step 2

cook the **soy-poached haddock**

1 (4-inch) piece unpeeled fresh gingerroot, sliced

1 cup reduced-sodium soy sauce

1 cup mirin

¹/₄ cup packed brown sugar

1¹/₂ pounds haddock fillets

1. Slice the ginger.

2. In a large, nonreactive Dutch oven, stir together the soy sauce, mirin, sugar, and ginger. Cover and bring to a boil over high heat. Reduce the heat to low.

3. Add the fish fillets, cover, and simmer gently for 3 minutes. Remove from the heat and let stand for 5 minutes, covered, or until ready to serve.

step 3

make the **steamed broccoli with sesame seeds**

12 ounces broccoli florets

1 teaspoon sesame seeds

Place broccoli florets in the steamer basket, cover, and steam until tender, 3 to 4 minutes. Put the broccoli in a serving bowl, sprinkle with salt to taste and 1 teaspoon sesame seeds and place on the table.

step 4

serve

1. Divide the rice among 4 plates. Lift fish out of poaching liquid and set on top of each serving. Spoon a little of the poaching liquid over each and serve with the broccoli.

2. When ready for dessert, place the clementines or orange wedges in a bowl and the fortune cookies on a plate. Serve.

Soy-Poached Haddock
Single serving is ¹/₄ of total recipe
CALORIES 395; PROTEIN 40g; CARBS 37g;
TOTAL FAT 1g; SAT FAT 0g; CHOLESTEROL 108mg;
SODIUM 2542mg; FIBER 0g

island-style orange roughy

chili-lime corn on the cob

coleslaw

quick strawberry shortcake

menu
gameplan

shopping list

Limes

Gingerroot

Apricot preserves

Orange roughy fillets

Pre-shucked corn on the cob

Coleslaw

Biscuits or individual
sponge cakes

Frozen strawberries in syrup

Canned refrigerated
whipped cream

from your pantry

Vegetable cooking spray

Soy sauce

Butter

Chili powder

Salt and pepper

serves 4

beforeyoustart

Thaw the strawberries according to
package directions. Preheat the broiler;
bring a large, shallow pot of water to a
boil, covered.

step **1** prepare the glaze for and
marinate the **island-
style orange roughy**

step **2** cook the **chili-lime
corn on the cob**

step **3** broil the **orange
roughy**

step **4** **serve**

luckyforyou The glaze on the fish is
made with unpeeled ginger
and an entire lime, which means less prep work for you.
Use young (spring) ginger, which has papery, almost sheer
skin, tender flesh, and a mild flavor. And don't be put off
by the slightly bitter lime rind; marmalade (which the glaze
resembles) generally contains whole fruit, and the apricot
preserves add the requisite sweetness. Rinse the lime
before using.

"Even fish-shy eaters adore the orange roughy. True, roughy is a mild fish, but it's the glaze that wins them over."

—minutemeals' chef Lisa

step 1

prepare the glaze for and marinate the **island-style orange roughy**

1 lime, rinsed and cut into quarters

1-inch knob unpeeled fresh gingerroot

2 tablespoons apricot preserves

2 tablespoons soy sauce

1 1/2 pounds orange roughy fillets

1. Preheat the broiler. Line the broiler pan with aluminum foil. Coat the broiler-pan rack with nonstick vegetable cooking spray.

2. Rinse the lime and cut it into quarters. Put the lime, ginger, apricot preserves, and soy sauce into a food processor and process until smooth.

3. Place the fish fillets in a glass baking dish large enough to hold them in a single layer. Spread some of the marinade on both sides of each fillet and set aside. Cover and let stand 5 minutes.

step 2

cook the **chili-lime corn on the cob**

4 ears pre-shucked corn on the cob

2 tablespoons butter, softened

1 lime

1 teaspoon chili powder

1. Bring a large shallow pot of water to a boil, covered, over high heat. Add the corn, cover, and cook 2 to 4 minutes, until just tender. Remove from the heat, leaving the corn in the hot water until ready to serve.

2. Place the butter in a small bowl. Squeeze in the juice from the lime. Add the chili powder and salt and pepper to taste and mash to combine. Set the bowl on the table.

step 3

broil the **orange roughy**

Transfer the fillets to the prepared broiler rack. Broil 3 to 5 inches from the heat for 4 to 6 minutes. Using a spatula, transfer 1 fillet to each of 4 dinner plates and bring to the table.

step 4

serve

1. Put the coleslaw in a serving bowl and place on the table.

2. Place an ear of corn next to the fish on each plate and pass the chili-lime butter.

3. When ready for dessert, split the biscuits and set a bottom on each of 4 dessert plates. Top each with some of the berries, their syrup, and whipped cream. Cover each with a biscuit top and serve. (Or, set a sponge cake on each of 4 dessert plates, fill the hollows with berries and syrup, and top with whipped cream.)

Island-Style Orange Roughy
Single serving is 1/4 of total recipe
CALORIES 149; PROTEIN 25g; CARBS 9g;
TOTAL FAT 1g; SAT FAT 0g; CHOLESTEROL 33mg;
SODIUM 622mg; FIBER 1g

pan-grilled salmon
with chipotle butter

couscous with toasted pine nuts

roast asparagus with lemon

coffee ice cream with espresso and cinnamon

menu
gameplan

shopping list

Couscous mix with toasted pine nuts

Asparagus

Salmon fillets

Chipotle in adobo sauce

Scallion

Coffee ice cream

Prepared espresso or strong coffee (takeout, about 1 cup)

from your pantry

Olive oil

Salt

Lemon (for juice)

Butter

Ground cumin

Freshly ground black pepper

Ground cinnamon

serves 4

beforeyou**start**

Preheat the oven to 475°F to roast the asparagus. Remove butter from the refrigerator to soften.

step **1** cook the **couscous with toasted pine nuts**

step **2** cook the **roast asparagus with lemon**

step **3** cook the **pan-grilled salmon with chipotle butter**

step **4** **serve**

lucky**for**you

Roasting intensifies the flavor of fresh asparagus to an extent that steaming and boiling just can't equal. It's a forgiving method, too: If you are roasting a main dish at a slightly lower temperature than we use here, just add a few minutes to the vegetable-cooking time and the results will be just as delicious.

"Maybe it's the asparagus, a true sign of spring, or the chipotles' warmth . . .This menu begs to be served alfresco." —minutemeals' chef Sarah

cook the **couscous with toasted pine nuts**

1 box (5.4 ounces) couscous mix with toasted pine nuts

Make the couscous with the amount of water and according to the directions on the package. Keep warm.

cook the **roast asparagus with lemon**

1 bunch (about 1¼ pounds) asparagus, trimmed (keep the rubber band around the bunch and trim as directed below)

1 tablespoon olive oil

1 tablespoon lemon juice (1 lemon)

1. Preheat the oven to 475°F. With the asparagus still bound by the rubber band, slice off about 1 inch of stalk from the end of the bunch. Remove the rubber band and place the asparagus on a jelly-roll or broiler pan. Drizzle with the oil and sprinkle with salt to taste. Toss to coat each stalk with oil and spread out in a single layer. Roast the asparagus until tender, 6 to 8 minutes.

2. Squeeze 1 tablespoon of lemon juice. Drizzle the juice over the asparagus.

cook the **pan-grilled salmon with chipotle butter**

3 tablespoons butter, softened

2 teaspoons ground cumin

4 salmon fillets, skinned (6 to 7 ounces and about 1 inch thick each)

1 small chipotle in adobo sauce, seeded and minced

1 scallion, finely chopped

1. Remove the butter from the refrigerator to soften. Place a grill pan over medium-high heat and heat for 2 to 3 minutes.

2. Mix the cumin with ¼ teaspoon each salt and pepper. Sprinkle the salmon with the spice mixture and press it into the flesh. Place the salmon skinned-side down in the heated grill-pan. Cook, turning once, 6 to 8 minutes.

3. Seed and mince the chipotle. Chop the scallion. In a small bowl, using a fork, work the chipotle and scallion into the softened butter.

serve

1. Fluff the couscous with a fork; turn into a serving bowl. Place the asparagus on a serving platter.

2. Place a salmon fillet on each of 4 dinner plates. Top each with a dollop of the chipotle butter.

3. When ready for dessert, scoop the coffee ice cream into 4 dessert dishes. Pour 3 to 4 tablespoons espresso or strong coffee over each scoop, and sprinkle with a dash of ground cinnamon.

Pan-Grilled Salmon with Chipotle Butter
Single serving is ¼ of total recipe

CALORIES 270; PROTEIN 32g; CARBS 1g; TOTAL FAT 14g; SAT FAT 6g; CHOLESTEROL 107mg; SODIUM 397mg; FIBER 1g

salmon and couscous in foil packets

stewed tomatoes and zucchini

blueberries with sour cream and brown sugar

shopping list

Couscous mix with wild mushrooms and herbs

Shallots

Salmon fillets

Lemon

Diced tomatoes with roasted garlic and onion

Frozen chopped green peppers

Zucchini

Blueberries

Sour cream, reduced-fat or regular

from your pantry

Dry white wine

Salt and pepper

Dried marjoram or basil

Brown sugar

serves 4

beforeyoustart

Preheat the oven to 425°F to bake the salmon and couscous.

step 1 cook the **salmon and couscous in foil packets**

step 2 make the **stewed tomatoes and zucchini**

step 3 prepare the **blueberries with sour cream and brown sugar**

step 4 serve

luckyforyou We can't overstate the appeal of cooking *en papillote*—the French technique of roasting foods in sealed packets of parchment paper or foil. The packets trap steam and natural juices, so fish and chicken cooked *en papillote* stay moist and juicy. You can vary the ingredients endlessly, and never add additional fat. Cleanup? Almost nonexistent.

"I almost feel guilty about this meal—it's wonderfully flavorful but you barely have to chop, stir, or clean up."

—minutemeals' chef Paul

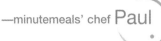

step 1

cook the **salmon and couscous in foil packets**

1/4 cup dry white wine

1 package (5.4 ounces) couscous mix with wild mushrooms and herbs

2 shallots, peeled and thinly sliced

4 salmon fillets (6 ounces each)

1 lemon, cut into wedges

1. Preheat the oven to 425°F. Tear off four 10-inch sheets of aluminum foil and lay them on a work surface.

2. In a liquid measuring cup stir together the 3/4 water, wine, and the contents of the seasoning packet. Slice the shallots.

3. Mound some of the dry couscous and shallots in the center of each piece of foil, dividing evenly. Place a salmon fillet on top of each mound and season with salt and pepper to taste. Working with 1 packet at time, gather the foil up around the mixture, without closing. Pour 1/4 cup of the seasoned water mixture into the packet and seal the top of the foil tightly. Place the packet on a jelly-roll pan or baking sheet. Repeat with the remaining packets.

4. Bake the salmon packets for 8 to 10 minutes or until the fish is just opaque in the thickest part. (Open a packet to check.)

step 2

while the salmon cooks, make the **stewed tomatoes and zucchini**

1 can (14 1/2 ounces) diced tomatoes with roasted garlic and onion

3/4 cup frozen chopped green peppers

1/2 teaspoon dried marjoram or basil

2 medium zucchini, trimmed

Place the tomatoes, green peppers, and marjoram in a heavy medium saucepan; cover, and bring to simmer. Meanwhile, cut each zucchini in half lengthwise and then thinly slice crosswise into half moons. Add to the simmering tomatoes, pressing down to submerge. Cover and cook for 8 minutes, or until zucchini is just tender. Season with salt and pepper to taste.

step 3

prepare the **blueberries with sour cream and brown sugar**

2 to 3 cups fresh blueberries, rinsed

1/2 cup reduced fat or regular sour cream

4 tablespoons brown sugar

1. Put the blueberries in a colander and rinse under cold running water. Pat dry with paper towels.

2. Divide the blueberries among 4 dessert bowls and refrigerate until serving.

step 4

serve

1. Place a fish packet on each of 4 dinner plates. Snip a vent hole to release any steam using kitchen scissors. Let each diner carefully open a packet (the mixture may steam). Pass the lemon wedges.

2. Divide the tomato and zucchini among 4 side dishes.

3. When ready for dessert, top each serving of blueberries with 2 tablespoons sour cream and 1 tablespoon brown sugar.

Salmon and Couscous in Foil Packets
Single serving is 1/4 of total recipe

CALORIES 330; PROTEIN 37g; CARBS 32g; TOTAL FAT 6g; SAT FAT 1g; CHOLESTEROL 83mg; SODIUM 554mg; FIBER 2g

hoisin-glazed salmon

sesame ramen noodles with vegetables

melon wedges with coconut macaroons

menu gameplan

shopping list

Salmon fillets

Gingerroot

Limes (for juice)

Hoisin sauce

Frozen broccoli or sugar-snap stir-fry mixture

Ramen noodles

Scallions

Cantaloupe or honeydew melon

Coconut macaroons

from your pantry

Cooking spray

Salt

Freshly ground black pepper

Soy sauce

Toasted sesame oil

Sesame seeds

serves 4

beforeyoustart

Preheat the broiler to cook the salmon. Bring the water to a boil in a large saucepan over high heat, covered.

| step | **1** | cook the **hoisin-glazed salmon** |

| step | **2** | cook the **sesame ramen noodles with vegetables** |

| step | **3** | assemble the **melon wedges with coconut macaroons** |

| step | **4** | **serve** |

headsup Be sure to brush the glaze on the salmon halfway through cooking, as directed. If you brush it on earlier, the sugar in the hoisin sauce caramelizes too quickly and then burns.

"I've heard hoisin sauce called ketchup for grownups. It's true. Taste the salmon and you'll be using hoisin again, and soon."

—minutemeals' chef Hillary

step 1

cook the **hoisin-glazed salmon**

4 salmon fillets (6 ounces each) with skin

1 (2-inch) piece fresh gingerroot, peeled and minced, about 2 tablespoons

3 tablespoons lime juice (2 limes)

1/4 cup hoisin sauce

2 tablespoons soy sauce

1. Preheat the broiler. Spray a broiler-pan rack with cooking spray. Line a broiler pan with aluminum foil. Place the fillets on the prepared pan and season with salt and pepper to taste. Broil 4 to 6 inches from the heat for 5 minutes.

2. Peel and mince the ginger. Squeeze enough lime juice to measure 3 tablespoons. In a small bowl, stir together the hoisin sauce, ginger, lime juice, and soy sauce. Spread over the salmon fillets and broil an additional 5 to 7 minutes or until the fish is opaque in the thickest part.

step 2

cook the **sesame ramen noodles with vegetables**

1 bag (16 ounces) frozen broccoli or sugar-snap stir-fry mixture

4 packages (3 ounces each) ramen noodles

2 teaspoons toasted sesame oil

1 tablespoon sesame seeds

4 scallions, thinly sliced on an angle

1. Pour 6 cups of water into a large saucepan, salt, cover, and bring to a boil over high heat. Add the frozen vegetables, cover, reduce the heat, and cook the vegetables for 6 to 8 minutes, stirring occasionally, until tender.

2. Discard the flavor packets from the noodles and add the noodles to the vegetables. Cook, uncovered, for 2 to 3 minutes, stirring occasionally. Drain. Transfer the vegetables and noodles to a serving bowl and toss with sesame oil, sesame seeds, and scallions. Season with salt and pepper to taste.

step 3

assemble the **melon wedges with coconut macaroons**

1 ripe cantaloupe or 1/2 ripe honeydew melon

Coconut macaroons

If using a whole melon, halve it. Scrape out seeds from the cantaloupe or honeydew melon halves and slice into wedges. Chill until serving time.

step 4

serve

1. Divide the noodles evenly among 4 bowls and top each serving with a piece of cooked salmon.

2. When ready for dessert, place a wedge of melon on each of 4 dessert plates, and serve with the coconut macaroons.

Hoisin-Glazed Salmon
Single serving is 1/4 of total recipe
CALORIES 298; PROTEIN 45g; CARBS 9g;
TOTAL FAT 8g; SAT FAT 1g; CHOLESTEROL 114mg;
SODIUM 1065mg; FIBER 1g

grilled swordfish
with lemon-rosemary butter

couscous with pimiento

steamed asparagus

lattice-top peach pie

menu
gameplan

---

shopping list

Fresh rosemary

Lemon (for juice)

Plain couscous

Pimiento

Asparagus

Swordfish steaks

Lattice-top peach pie

from your pantry

Butter

Salt and pepper

Fat-free reduced-sodium chicken broth

Olive oil

serves 4

beforeyoustart

Preheat the barbecue grill, if using.

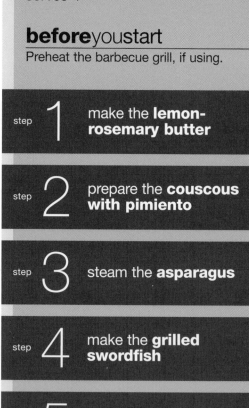

step **1** make the **lemon-rosemary butter**

step **2** prepare the **couscous with pimiento**

step **3** steam the **asparagus**

step **4** make the **grilled swordfish**

step **5** **serve**

headsup There is fresh swordfish and frozen and the prices are not the same, the fresh being considerably more expensive. Try both and see which best suits your taste.

"This is a birthday-dinner menu. Swordfish is special and so is asparagus—the flavors are fresh, the colors are lovely."

—minutemeals' chef Hillary

step 1

make the **lemon-rosemary butter**

1½ teaspoons fresh rosemary leaves

3 tablespoons fresh lemon juice (1 large lemon)

3 tablespoons butter, softened

1. Strip enough leaves from a branch of rosemary to measure 1½ teaspoons. Coarsely chop and place in a small bowl.

2. Squeeze 3 tablespoons fresh lemon juice into the bowl and add the butter. Mash with the back of a spoon until completely combined, almost fluffy. Season with salt and pepper to taste.

step 2

prepare the **couscous with pimiento**

2 cups fat-free reduced-sodium chicken broth

1½ cups plain couscous

3 tablespoons drained chopped pimiento

Bring the chicken broth to a boil, covered, in a 1-quart saucepan over high heat. Stir in the couscous, pimiento, and salt and pepper to taste. Cover and remove the pan from the heat. Let stand for 5 minutes.

step 3

steam the **asparagus**

1 pound pencil-thin asparagus

1. Snap off the end of each stalk of asparagus where it naturally breaks. Put the stalks in a steamer basket.

2. Put 1 inch of water in a saucepan large enough to hold the steamer basket. Place the basket in the pan, cover, and bring the water to a boil over high heat. Steam for 3 minutes, or until the stalks are crisp-tender when tested with a fork. Transfer the asparagus to a plate, season with salt and pepper to taste, and keep warm, loosely covered.

step 4

grill the **swordfish**

4 thin-to-medium-thick swordfish steaks (6 ounces each)

1 tablespoon olive oil

1. Preheat the barbecue grill or a grill pan over high heat until hot.

2. Rinse the swordfish steak and pat dry. Brush on both sides with the olive oil and season with salt and pepper to taste. Grill 3 to 5 minutes on each side, or until opaque when tested with a fork.

step 5

serve

1. Transfer each of the swordfish steaks to a large dinner plate. Immediately top each with 1 tablespoon of the lemon-rosemary butter and let it melt over the top.

2. Fluff the couscous with a fork. Divide the couscous among 4 plates and add a serving of asparagus to each. Serve at once.

3. When ready for dessert, cut the pie into slices and serve.

Grilled Swordfish with Lemon-Rosemary Butter
Single serving is ¼ of total recipe
CALORIES 317; PROTEIN 34g; CARBS 1g; TOTAL FAT 19g; SAT FAT 2g; CHOLESTEROL 89mg; SODIUM 153mg; FIBER 0g

trout with almonds

dilled yellow rice
goat cheese salad
chocolate sorbet
with fresh cherries

shopping list

Yellow rice mix

Fresh dill

Roasted red peppers

Goat cheese

Prewashed mixed
baby greens

Red wine vinaigrette
salad dressing

Trout fillets

Slivered almonds

Lemon

Chocolate sorbet

Cherries

from your pantry

Butter

Salt

Freshly ground black pepper

Olive oil

serves 4

beforeyoustart

Preheat the oven to 250°F to hold the
cooked fish. Rinse and chill the cherries.

step **1** make the **dilled
yellow rice**

step **2** assemble the **goat
cheese salad**

step **3** make the **trout with
almonds**

step **4** **serve**

headsup If cooked correctly, the trout
comes out of the pan with
beautifully crisp skin. Keep in mind two rules for success-
ful pan-frying: First, preheat the pan—you should hear
sizzle when you add the fillets. Second, don't crowd the
pan, or the trout will steam and turn soft. The fillets cook
so quickly that you can sauté them in two batches and
still complete the menu in 20 minutes.

"I first made this classic dish in cooking school. The trio of trout, almonds, and butter still thrills me."

—minutemeals' chef

step 1
make the **dilled yellow rice**

2 boxes (4 ounces each) 10-minute yellow rice mix

1 tablespoon butter

2 tablespoons snipped fresh dill

Make the rice in the amount of water and for the time directed on the package, using the tablespoon of butter. Snip enough dill to measure 2 tablespoons, and stir into the cooked rice. Cover to keep warm.

step 2
assemble the **goat cheese salad**

1/3 cup roasted red pepper

1 log (4 ounces) goat cheese

1 bag (5 ounces) prewashed mixed baby greens

1/4 cup red wine vinaigrette salad dressing

1. Drain the peppers and cut them into thin strips. Slice the goat cheese into thin rounds.

2. Pour the dressing into the bottom of a salad bowl. Cross 2 large serving utensils over the dressing. Place the greens, red pepper strips, and goat cheese on top of the crossed utensils. Put the salad on the table; do not toss.

step 3
make the **trout with almonds**

8 trout fillets (about 2 pounds, 4 ounces each)

1/4 cup slivered almonds

2 tablespoons butter

2 tablespoons olive oil

Lemon wedges (optional)

1. Preheat the oven to 250°F. Rinse the fish and pat dry. Season the trout fillets with salt and pepper to taste.

2. Heat a large heavy skillet over medium heat. Add the almonds and cook 2 minutes, stirring constantly, until golden. Tip out of the pan and onto a plate.

3. Return the skillet to the burner and increase the heat to medium-high. Add 1 tablespoon butter and 1 tablespoon olive oil and heat until the butter melts. Add 4 of the trout fillets, skin side down, taking care not to crowd the pan. Cook about 5 minutes, turning once, until the fillets are just opaque in the thickest part. Transfer the fillets to a serving platter and place in the oven to keep warm. Without wiping out the pan, repeat with the remaining butter, oil, and fish, if necessary. When the second batch is done, sprinkle the fillets with the almonds. (If you have 2 large heavy skillets, you can cook all of the trout at once, dividing the ingredients evenly between the pans.)

step 4
serve

1. Toss the salad, season with salt and pepper to taste, and toss again.

2. Fluff the rice with a fork. Place a fillet and a lemon wedge, if using, on each of 4 dinner plates and spoon some rice alongside.

3. When ready for dessert, scoop the sorbet into 4 bowls and bring to the table. Pass the chilled cherries.

Trout with Almonds
Single serving is 1/4 of total recipe
CALORIES 523; PROTEIN 54g; CARBS 1g; TOTAL FAT 33g; SAT FAT 8g; CHOLESTEROL 161mg; SODIUM 336mg; FIBER 1g

tuna pita melts
vegetable chips
three-bean salads
raspberry–banana compote and chocolate cream wafers

shopping list

Pita pockets (6-inch diameter)

Canned water-packed tuna

Pimiento

Shredded Mexican
or taco-blend cheese

Boston lettuce

Three-bean salad
(from the salad bar,
deli counter, or canned)

Vegetable chips

Quick-thaw frozen raspberries

Bananas

Chocolate cream wafers

from your pantry

Mayonnaise

Salt and pepper

luckyforyou This sandwich supper is
meant to be easy, but that
doesn't mean you can't jazz it up each time you make it.
Instead of plain pita bread, try garlic or onion- and herb-
seasoned; top the sandwiches with thin slices of Swiss
cheese or an Italian-style shredded cheese blend.

menu
gameplan

serves 4

beforeyoustart
Preheat the oven to 400°F. Chill the
bean salad. Thaw the frozen raspberries.

step **1** prepare the **tuna pita melts**

step **2** assemble the **three-bean salads**

step **3** prepare the **dessert**

step **4** **serve**

"Add a bowl of tomato soup, and you've got the meal that sustained me through childhood."

—minutemeals' chef Ruth

step 1

prepare the **tuna pita melts**

4 pita pockets (6-inch diameter)

2 cans (6 ounces each) water-packed tuna

2 to 3 tablespoons chopped pimiento

1/3 cup mayonnaise

1 1/3 cups packaged shredded Mexican or taco blend cheese

1. Preheat the oven to 400°F. Place the pita pockets on a baking sheet and warm for 5 minutes while preparing filling.

2. Drain the tuna and place in a small bowl. Flake the tuna with a fork and stir in the pimiento and mayonnaise. Season with salt and pepper to taste. Divide the tuna mixture among the heated pita rounds, spreading evenly to within 1/2 inch from the edge. Sprinkle with the cheese.

3. Bake the tuna melts for 5 to 7 minutes, until the cheese is melted and beginning to bubble.

step 2

assemble the **three-bean salads**

1 small head Boston lettuce

1 pound fresh three-bean salad, or 1 can (15 ounces) three-bean salad

1. Separate the head of lettuce into 4 cups. Rinse and pat dry with paper towels.

2. Place a large lettuce-leaf cup on each of 4 dinner plates. Spoon some of the bean salad into each lettuce cup.

step 3

prepare the **raspberry-banana compote and chocolate cream wafers**

1 package (10 ounces) quick-thaw frozen raspberries

2 small bananas

Chocolate cream wafers

1. Thaw raspberries as directed on package and place in a small bowl.

2. Thinly slice the bananas and combine with the berries, making sure that bananas are covered with syrup to prevent browning. Place in the refrigerator until serving.

step 4

serve

1. Place vegetable chips in a napkin-lined basket. Place on table.

2. Place a heated tuna pita melt on each dinner plate next to the 4 bean salad cups; serve.

3. When ready for dessert, divide the compote among 4 dessert dishes. Serve with the chocolate cream wafers.

Tuna Pita Melts
Single serving is 1/4 of total recipe
CALORIES 521; PROTEIN 31g; CARBS 35g;
TOTAL FAT 28g; SAT FAT 11g; CHOLESTEROL 74mg;
SODIUM 1078mg; FIBER 2g

sautéed scallops

greens and mushroom salad
baguette rounds
with flavored cheese
poire brûlée

shopping list

Baguette

Spreadable herb and garlic
cheese (such as Boursin or
Rondele)

Canned pear halves
in light syrup

Vanilla ice cream

Red pepper slices
(from the salad bar)

Mushroom slices
(from the produce department)

Raspberry vinaigrette
salad dressing

Prewashed European
salad mix

Sea scallops

Fresh chives or scallions

from your pantry

Brown sugar

All-purpose flour

Butter

Salt and pepper

Olive oil

serves 4

beforeyoustart

Preheat the broiler to cook the pears.

step 1 prepare the **baguette rounds with flavored cheese**

step 2 prepare the **poire brûlée**

step 3 assemble the **greens and mushroom salad**

step 4 make the **sautéed scallops**

step 5 serve

headsup

Like all fish and seafood, scallops should be purchased when absolutely fresh. One way to guarantee that they are is to buy them from a trusted source, be it your local fish market or a supermarket with knowledgeable staff and a quality seafood department. Try to buy loose scallops—you want to make sure they smell sweet, not fishy, and you can't sniff if they are already wrapped in plastic.

"Scallops are my weeknight-dinner-party secret weapon. They're so special but they don't tie me to the kitchen."

—minutemeals' chef Patty

step 1

prepare the **baguette rounds with flavored cheese**

1 baguette (about 12 ounces)

1 container (Boursin is 5.2 ounces, Rondele is 4) spreadable herb and garlic cheese

Slice the baguette into 16 thin slices, about $3/4$ inch thick. Spread each slice with some of the cheese. Arrange on a serving platter and place on the table.

step 2

prepare the **poire brûlée**

8 pear halves in light syrup

2 tablespoons brown sugar

1 tablespoon all-purpose flour

2 tablespoons cold butter, cut into bits

1 pint vanilla ice cream

1. Preheat the broiler. Line a broiler-pan rack with a sheet of aluminum foil.

2. Drain the pears. Arrange them cut-side-up on the prepared broiler pan.

3. In small bowl, using your fingers or a fork, work the brown sugar and flour into the butter until crumbly. Sprinkle evenly over the pear halves.

step 3

assemble the **greens and mushroom salad**

1 cup red pepper slices

1 cup mushroom slices

$1/4$ cup raspberry vinaigrette salad dressing

1 bag (5 ounces) prewashed European salad mix

Coarsely chop the red pepper slices and place in a salad bowl. Add the mushrooms, vinaigrette, and salt and pepper to taste. Mix well. Place the greens on top. Do not toss; place the bowl on the table.

step 4

make the **sautéed scallops**

$1 1/4$ pounds sea scallops

1 tablespoon olive oil

2 tablespoons snipped fresh chives or scallion greens

1. Season the scallops with $1/4$ teaspoon salt and $1/8$ teaspoon pepper.

2. Heat the oil in a large nonstick skillet over medium-high heat. Add the scallops and cook, turning once, for 3 minutes, or until the scallops are opaque in the center and slightly golden.

3. Transfer the scallops to 4 dinner plates, dividing evenly. Snip enough chives or scallion greens to measure 2 tablespoons and sprinkle over each serving. Place the plates on the table.

step 5

serve

1. Toss the salad and serve with the scallops. Pass the baguette rounds.

2. When ready for dessert, broil the pears for 2 minutes or until the butter mixture is bubbly. Serve with a scoop of vanilla ice cream.

Sautéed Scallops
Single serving is $1/4$ of total recipe
CALORIES 106; PROTEIN 12g; CARBS 2g;
TOTAL FAT 6g; SAT FAT 1g; CHOLESTEROL 23mg;
SODIUM 276mg; FIBER 0g

crunchy cumin shrimp

corn chips with bean and corn salsa

tomato, orange, and red onion salad

lemon pound cake with glaze

menu gameplan

shopping list

Limes (for juice and wedges)

Lemon pound cake

Tomatoes

Canned mandarin oranges

Red onion slices
(from the salad bar)

Large shrimp,
peeled and deveined

Corn chips

Bean and corn salsa

from your pantry

Confectioners' sugar

Salt

Freshly ground black pepper

Olive oil

Sherry vinegar

Whole cumin seeds

Cayenne pepper

serves 4

beforeyoustart
Preheat the broiler to cook the shrimp.

step 1 make the **lemon pound cake with glaze**

step 2 assemble the **tomato, orange, and red onion salad**

step 3 make the **crunchy cumin shrimp**

step 4 serve

headsup It's best to buy spices, whole and ground, in small amounts; say, not much more than you'll use in 6 months. After that time, the flavors start to fade. (Store spices in tightly closed containers in a cool, dark place.)

"Cumin seeds, not ground cumin, are the real surprise element here. They crunch when you bite into the shrimp."

—minutemeals' chef Wendy

step 1
make the **lemon pound cake with glaze**

1 1/2 tablespoons lime juice (1 lime)

1 cup confectioners' sugar

4 slices lemon pound cake

1. Squeeze the lime to make 1 1/2 tablespoons of juice. Place the sugar in a small bowl and mix in the lime juice until smooth.

2. Place a piece of cake on each of 4 dessert plates and drizzle some of the glaze over each. Let stand until ready to serve.

step 2
assemble the **tomato, orange, and red onion salad**

3 ripe medium tomatoes

1 can (11 ounces) mandarin oranges, drained

1/4 cup red onion slices

1 tablespoon olive oil

1 teaspoon sherry vinegar

Slice the tomatoes. Arrange the slices, overlapping them slightly, on a platter. Scatter the orange slices and red onion over the tomatoes. Season with salt and pepper to taste. Drizzle with the olive oil and sherry vinegar. Place the platter on the table.

step 3
make the **crunchy cumin shrimp**

4 teaspoons whole cumin seeds

2 tablespoons olive oil

1/4 teaspoon cayenne pepper

1 1/2 pounds peeled and deveined large shrimp

1 lime, cut into wedges

1. Preheat the broiler.

2. On a cutting board moisten the cumin seeds with a bit of olive oil and chop coarsely with a chef's knife. In a medium bowl mix the chopped cumin with the remaining oil, the cayenne pepper, and salt to taste. Toss the shrimp in the seasoned oil until well coated.

3. Spread the shrimp on a jelly-roll pan. Broil 4 inches from the heat for 4 minutes, turning once, until the shrimp are pink and firm. Cut the lime into wedges. Mound the shrimp on a serving platter and arrange the lime wedges around the shrimp. Place the platter on the table.

step 4
serve

1. Place the corn chips in a basket and the bean and corn salsa in a small serving bowl. Bring them to the table and serve with the cumin shrimp and the tomato salad.

2. When ready for dessert, serve the glazed pound cake.

Crunchy Cumin Shrimp
Single serving is 1/4 of total recipe
CALORIES 190; PROTEIN 26g; CARBS 1g;
TOTAL FAT 9g; SAT FAT 1g; CHOLESTEROL 242mg;
SODIUM 426mg; FIBER 0g

teriyaki shrimp

tropical brown rice

micro-steamed snow peas

coconut sorbet with
lemon nut shortbread

menu
gameplan

serves 4

step **1** make the **tropical brown rice**

step **2** cook the **teriyaki shrimp**

step **3** make the **micro-steamed snow peas**

step **4** serve

shopping list

Canned tropical fruit salad

Large shrimp, peeled and deveined

Pineapple all-fruit spread

Pre-chopped ginger (from the produce section)

Fresh snow or sugar-snap peas

Coconut sorbet

Lemon nut shortbread

from your pantry

Instant brown rice

Salt and pepper

Olive oil

Reduced-sodium teriyaki sauce

Butter

luckyforyou

This menu is completely forgiving of last-minute substitutions: If the shrimp at your supermarket aren't fresh, substitute chicken tenders, increasing the cooking time to 7 or 8 minutes. If you can't find pineapple all-fruit spread, apricot will be just fine. The important thing is to use a spread sweetened only with fruit juice; regular jam or jelly is too sweet to use here.

"I'm always looking for ways to streamline dinner. I was thrilled to discover pre-chopped ginger—Asian cooking just got easier."

—minutemeals' chef Patty

step 1

make the **tropical brown rice**

2 cups instant brown rice

1 can (20 ounces) tropical fruit salad, drained

1. Prepare the rice in the amount of water and for the time directed on the package.

2. Drain the fruit salad and stir into the cooked rice. Cover to keep warm.

step 2

cook the **teriyaki shrimp**

1¹/2 pounds peeled and deveined large shrimp

1 tablespoon olive oil

¹/2 cup pineapple all-fruit spread

2 teaspoons pre-chopped ginger

¹/4 cup reduced-sodium teriyaki sauce

1. Season the shrimp with ¹/4 teaspoon salt and ¹/8 teaspoon pepper.

2. Heat the oil in a large nonstick skillet over medium-high heat. Add the shrimp and cook, stirring often, for 2 to 3 minutes, or until the shrimp turn pink.

3. Meanwhile, stir together the pineapple all-fruit, ginger, and teriyaki sauce in a small bowl.

4. Add the pineapple mixture to the shrimp and cook for 2 to 3 minutes, tossing, until the shrimp are nicely glazed and the sauce is bubbling.

step 3

make the **micro-steamed snow peas**

12 ounces snow or sugar-snap peas, pretrimmed, if possible

1 tablespoon butter

1. Trim the snow peas, if necessary. Put the snow peas in a microwave-safe dish large enough to hold them in almost a single layer. Drizzle with 2 tablespoons water and cover with a lid or vented plastic wrap. Microwave on High for 2 to 4 minutes, until bright green and crisp-tender.

2. Drain the snow peas and place in a serving bowl. Toss with the butter and salt and pepper to taste.

step 4

serve

1. Divide the tropical rice among 4 dinner plates.

2. Top each serving with some of the teriyaki shrimp and snow peas, drizzling any sauce remaining in the shrimp-cooking pan over all.

3. When ready for dessert, scoop the coconut sorbet into 4 dessert bowls and serve with the lemon nut shortbread cookies.

Teriyaki Shrimp
Single serving is ¹/4 of total recipe
CALORIES 249; PROTEIN 27g; CARBS 23g;
TOTAL FAT 5g; SAT FAT 1g; CHOLESTEROL 242mg;
SODIUM 744mg; FIBER 0g

fish stew
with orange and fennel
pear and gorgonzola salad
sourdough rolls
marble pound cake
with chocolate drizzle

serves 4

step 1 cook the **fish stew with orange and fennel**

step 2 make the **pear and gorgonzola salad**

step 3 prepare the **marble pound cake with chocolate drizzle**

step 4 serve

shopping list

Italian-style stewed tomatoes

Fennel bulb

Orange

Fish cubes for kabobs
or cod fillet

Fresh basil

Prewashed salad greens mix

Canned pear halves in juice

Crumbled Gorgonzola cheese

Chopped hazelnuts
or slivered almonds

Citrus vinaigrette
salad dressing

Pound cake

Hot fudge sauce

Sourdough rolls

from your pantry

Salt and pepper

luckyforyou

Many large supermarkets now sell fish cut specifically for using on kabobs. Note, though, that some packages of pre-cubed fish may contain more than one species, some firmer than cod, like swordfish, that will require an additional cooking time of 3 to 4 minutes. If your supermarket does not carry precut fish, ask your fishmonger to cube some cod for you.

"This is a sunny, sophisticated stew. The combination of fennel and orange brings complexity to an otherwise humble dish." —minutemeals' chef Paul

step 1

cook the **fish stew with orange and fennel**

2 cans (14½ ounces each) Italian-style stewed tomatoes

1 small fennel bulb

1 large navel orange

1 pound fish cubes for kabobs or 1 pound cod fillet, cut into 1 inch pieces

⅓ cup fresh basil leaves

1. Place the tomatoes and ⅓ cup water in a large saucepan, cover, and bring to a boil over high heat. Quarter the fennel bulb lengthwise, cut out the core, and thinly slice the fennel crosswise. With a vegetable peeler, remove two 2-inch strips of peel from the orange. Add the fennel and orange peel to the tomatoes; halve the orange and squeeze the juice into the pan, being careful not to add the seeds. Bring to a boil, cover, reduce the heat slightly, and simmer for 8 minutes.

2. Stir the fish cubes into the stew, pushing down to submerge. Cover, reduce the heat, and simmer for 3 to 5 minutes or until the fish is opaque. While the fish simmers, cut the basil into slivers. Stir in the basil and season with pepper to taste. Cover and remove from the heat.

step 2

while the stew cooks, make the **pear and gorgonzola salad**

1 package (10 ounces) prewashed salad greens mix

1 can (15 ounces) pear halves in juice, drained

½ cup crumbled Gorgonzola cheese

⅓ cup chopped hazelnuts or slivered almonds

⅓ cup citrus vinaigrette salad dressing

Place the salad greens in a salad bowl. Slice the pears and scatter the slices over the greens. Top with the Gorgonzola and hazelnuts. Add the dressing, season with salt and pepper to taste, and toss to mix. Place the bowl on the table with 4 salad plates.

step 3

prepare the **marble pound cake with chocolate drizzle**

1 marble or plain pound cake, thawed if frozen

⅓ cup jarred hot fudge sauce

Cut the pound cake into six ¾-inch-thick slices. Cut each slice in half on the diagonal. Arrange 3 triangles of cake on each of 4 dessert plates. Place the hot fudge sauce in a microwave-safe container.

step 4

serve

1. Place the rolls in a napkin-lined basket.

2. Remove the strips of orange peel from the stew, ladle the stew into 4 bowls, and serve with the salad and the rolls.

3. When ready for dessert, microwave the fudge sauce on High for 30 seconds. Drizzle over the pound cake slices and serve.

Fish Stew with Orange and Fennel
Single serving is ¼ of total recipe
CALORIES 129; PROTEIN 15g; CARBS 19g; TOTAL FAT 1g; SAT FAT 0g; CHOLESTEROL 30mg; SODIUM 739mg; FIBER 5g

minute
5-ingredient

pasta and grains
menus

meals

main dishes

spinach fettuccine
with bolognese sauce

salad with gorgonzola-tomato dressing

garlic-herb rolls

cappuccino gelato with chocolate-filled cookies

menu
gameplan

shopping list

Ground meatloaf mix

Fresh basil

Crusty rolls

Salt-free garlic-herb seasoning

Tomato

Creamy Italian salad dressing

Crumbled Gorgonzola cheese

Prewashed spring salad greens mix

Fresh refrigerated spinach fettuccine

Cappuccino gelato or coffee ice cream

Chocolate-filled cookies (such as Milano)

from your pantry

Salt

Spicy pasta sauce

Butter

Grated Parmesan cheese

Freshly ground black pepper

serves 4

beforeyoustart

Preheat the oven to 450°F. Bring the water to a boil in a large pot, covered.

step **1** cook the **bolognese sauce**

step **2** warm the **garlic-herb rolls**

step **3** assemble the **salad with gorgonzola-tomato dressing**

step **4** cook the **spinach fettuccine**

step **5** **serve**

luckyforyou
The three ground meats that give body and flavor to classic Bolognese sauce—lean beef, pork, and veal—are available packaged together and labeled as meatloaf mix.

"Traditional Bolognese sauce simmers for hours; mine takes minutes. Herbs and cheese give it the depth of slow-cooked sauce."

—minutemeals' chef Sarah

step 1
cook the **bolognese sauce**

1 pound ground meatloaf mix

1 jar (26 ounces) spicy pasta sauce

1 cup lightly packed basil, chopped

3/4 cup grated Parmesan cheese

1. Pour 4 quarts of water into a large pot, salt lightly, and cover. Bring to a boil over high heat.

2. Heat a large heavy skillet over medium-high heat. Crumble the meatloaf mix into the skillet, increase the heat to high, and cook, stirring to break up chunks, until the meat is no longer pink, about 4 minutes.

3. Stir the pasta sauce into the meat. Reduce the heat and simmer for 10 minutes.

4. Chop the basil. Remove the sauce from the heat and stir in the basil and Parmesan cheese.

step 2
warm the **garlic-herb rolls**

4 small crusty rolls, split

2 tablespoons butter, softened

2 tablespoons grated Parmesan cheese

1 teaspoon salt-free garlic-herb seasoning blend

1. Preheat the oven to 450°F. Split the rolls. Combine the butter, Parmesan cheese, and garlic-herb seasoning in a small bowl. Mash with a fork until blended.

2. Spread the cut sides of the rolls with the butter mixture. Place cut side up on a baking sheet. Bake until hot and lightly browned at the edges, 4 to 5 minutes.

step 3
assemble the **salad with gorgonzola-tomato dressing**

1 small tomato, diced

1/4 cup creamy Italian salad dressing

2 tablespoons crumbled Gorgonzola cheese

1 bag (5 ounces) prewashed spring salad greens mix

Dice the tomato. Combine the tomato, salad dressing, and Gorgonzola cheese in a salad bowl. Toss well, season with pepper to taste, and toss again. Place the greens on top of the tomato and cheese mixture; do not toss. Place the bowl on the table with 4 salad plates.

step 4
cook the **spinach fettuccine**

12 ounces fresh spinach fettuccine

Add the pasta to the boiling water and cook according to the package directions, until *al dente*, stirring once or twice. Drain. Add the pasta to the sauce and toss to combine.

step 5
serve

1. Divide the pasta among 4 serving bowls. Pass the remaining Parmesan cheese.

2. Toss the salad and serve with the pasta and rolls.

3. When ready for dessert, scoop the gelato or ice cream into 4 dessert dishes and serve with the chocolate-filled cookies.

Spinach Fettuccine with Spicy Bolognese Sauce
Single serving is 1/4 of total recipe
CALORIES 246; PROTEIN 27g; CARBS 15g; TOTAL FAT 9g; SAT FAT 2g; CHOLESTEROL 63mg; SODIUM 525mg; FIBER 3g

garlic and parsley pasta
with shrimp

greens and spinach salad

whole-grain italian bread

fresh cherries with chocolate wafer cookies

menu gameplan

shopping list

Prewashed mixed
salad greens

Prewashed spinach

Cucumber slices
(from the salad bar)

Halved cherry tomatoes
(from the salad bar)

Garlic and parsley pasta

Large shrimp, peeled and
deveined

Roasted peppers with garlic

Clam juice or fat-free reduced-
sodium chicken broth

Crusty whole-grain
Italian bread

Cherries

Chocolate wafer cookies

from your pantry

Vinaigrette salad dressing,
store-bought

Salt

Olive oil

Freshly ground black pepper

serves 4

beforeyoustart

Bring the water to a boil in a large pot,
covered. Rinse and chill the cherries.

step 1 prepare the **greens and spinach salad**

step 2 cook the **garlic and parsley pasta with shrimp**

step 3 **serve**

luckyforyou

Flavored pasta is increasingly popular, and that's no surprise. The flavorings—like herbs, garlic, black pepper, Parmesan, tomato—are just the ingredients that you might add to homemade pasta sauce. With flavored pasta, you're saved the trouble of preparing those ingredients yourself. You'll notice too how pretty many of the pastas are. You can find flavored pasta in both the dried and refrigerated fresh pasta sections of most supermarkets.

"The shrimp make this dish really special and festive, but you can substitute chicken tenders if you like."

—minutemeals' chef Hillary

step 1

prepare the **greens and spinach salad**

- 4 cups prewashed mixed salad greens
- 2 cups prewashed spinach
- 1 cup cucumber slices
- 1/2 cup halved cherry tomatoes
- 2 to 4 tablespoons prepared vinaigrette salad dressing

Combine the salad greens, spinach, cucumber slices, and tomatoes in a large salad bowl. Put the bowl on the table with the vinaigrette dressing and 4 salad plates.

step 2

cook the **garlic and parsley pasta with shrimp**

- 2 packages (8 ounces each) garlic and parsley pasta
- 1/4 cup olive oil
- 1 1/2 pounds peeled and deveined large shrimp
- 1 cup roasted peppers with garlic, drained and chopped
- 1 cup clam juice or fat-free reduced-sodium chicken broth

1. Cook the pasta: Pour 4 quarts water into a large pot, salt lightly, and cover. Bring to a boil over high heat. Add the pasta and cook according to the directions on the package, until *al dente*. Drain in a colander.

2. Make the sauce: Heat the oil in the pasta cooking pot over medium-high heat. Add the shrimp, season lightly with salt and pepper, and cook 2 to 3 minute, stirring occasionally, until most of the shrimp turns pink.

3. Coarsely chop the roasted peppers. Add the peppers to the shrimp and cook 1 minute longer, stirring. Add the clam juice, cover, bring to a boil, and remove from the heat. Add the pasta and toss to mix well. Divide the pasta among 4 bowls and bring to the table.

step 3

serve

1. Place the whole-grain Italian bread on a cutting board with a serrated knife and bring them to the table.

2. Toss the salad with the vinaigrette, season with salt and pepper, and serve with the pasta.

3. When ready for dessert, place the cherries on the table, with a small bowl for pits, and serve with the chocolate wafer cookies.

Garlic and Parsley Pasta with Shrimp
Single serving is 1/4 of total recipe
CALORIES 661; PROTEIN 42g; CARBS 88g;
TOTAL FAT 16g; SAT FAT 2g; CHOLESTEROL 242mg;
SODIUM 931mg; FIBER 4g

pasta marinara
with tuna, peas, and olives

spinach and mushroom salad

crisp sesame flatbreads

watermelon chunks with amaretti cookies

menu
gameplan

shopping list

Capellini

Frozen baby peas

Canned water-packed tuna

Canned sliced pitted ripe olives

Prewashed baby spinach

Mushroom slices (from the produce department)

Red onion slices (from the salad bar)

Italian salad dressing

Crisp sesame flatbreads

Watermelon chunks (from the produce department)

Amaretti cookies

from your pantry

Salt

Jarred tomato pasta sauce

Freshly ground black pepper

serves 4

beforeyoustart

Bring the water to a boil in a large pot of salted water, covered. Chill the watermelon chunks.

step 1 cook the **pasta marinara with tuna, peas, and olives**

step 2 assemble the **spinach and mushroom salad**

step 3 serve

headsup
Cooking the peas in the pasta water rather than heating them in the marinara sauce is the trick that keeps them a sprightly green, so the finished dish is as visually appealing as it is delicious.

"It's OK to break the rule against serving Parmesan cheese with seafood sauce. If you like the combination, that's what counts."

—minutemeals' chef Ruth

step 1
cook the **pasta marinara with tuna, peas, and olives**

12 ounces capellini

1 package (10 ounces) frozen baby peas

2 cans (6 ounces each) water-packed tuna, drained and flaked

2 cups jarred tomato pasta sauce

1/2 cup sliced pitted ripe olives

1. Cook the pasta: Pour 4 quarts water into a large pot, salt lightly, and cover. Bring to a boil over high heat. Stir in the pasta and frozen peas. Cook, stirring often, 4 to 5 minutes, until pasta is *al dente* and the peas just tender. Drain pasta and peas in a colander and return to the cooking pot. Cover to keep warm.

2. While the pasta cooks, make the sauce: Drain and flake the tuna, and place in a heavy medium saucepan. Stir in the pasta sauce and sliced olives. Place over low heat, cover, and bring to a simmer, stirring occasionally.

step 2
assemble the **spinach and mushroom salad**

1 bag (about 5 ounces) prewashed baby spinach

1 cup mushroom slices

1/4 cup red onion slices

1/4 cup Italian salad dressing

Place the spinach, mushrooms, and red onion slices in a salad bowl. Sprinkle with the salad dressing and pepper to taste. Toss the salad and place on the table with 4 salad plates.

step 3
serve

1. Place the sesame flatbreads in a napkin-lined basket.

2. Add the hot sauce to the pasta and toss well. Divide among 4 serving bowls and serve with the salad.

3. When ready for dessert, place the chilled watermelon chunks on the table and serve with the cookies.

Pasta Marinara with Tuna, Peas, and Olives
Single serving is 1/4 of total recipe

CALORIES 584; PROTEIN 34g; CARBS 91g;
TOTAL FAT 10g; SAT FAT 2g; CHOLESTEROL 30mg;
SODIUM 1499mg; FIBER 9g

spaghetti amatriciana

hearts of romaine salad with olives and marinated vegetables

sesame seed breadsticks

crumb cake with red grapes

menu gameplan

serves 4

beforeyoustart

Bring the water to a boil in a large pot, covered. Rinse and chill the grapes.

step 1 cook the **spaghetti amatriciana**

step 2 prepare the **salad**

step 3 **serve**

---

shopping list

Spaghetti

Thick-cut bacon

Onion slices
(from the salad bar)

Diced tomatoes with
balsamic vinegar, basil,
and olive oil, Hunt's brand

Prewashed chopped
romaine mix

Jarred roasted red peppers
with garlic

Giardiniera (Italian marinated
vegetables salad, jarred or
from the deli department)

Pitted kalamata olives

Sesame seed breadsticks

Red seedless grapes
(from the salad bar)

Crumb cake

from your pantry

Salt

Crushed red pepper flakes

Olive oil

Freshly ground black pepper

headsup

Buy more olives, roasted peppers, and giardiniera than you need for the salad here. Whatever you don't use can be chopped together and used as a topping on toasted Italian bread for pre-dinner nibbles throughout the week.

"This is a spur-of-the-moment meal. Look at the shopping list—nearly everything can be kept in your pantry."

—minutemeals' chef Lisa

step 1

cook the **spaghetti amatriciana**

- 1 pound spaghetti
- 4 slices thick-cut bacon
- 1 1/2 cups onion slices
- 2 cans (14 1/2 ounces each) Hunt's diced tomatoes with balsamic vinegar, basil and olive oil
- Crushed red pepper flakes to taste

1. Cook the pasta: Pour 4 quarts water into a large pot, salt lightly, and cover. Bring to a boil over high heat. Add the spaghetti and cook according to the directions on the package, until *al dente*. Drain in a colander. Return the pasta to the pot. Cover to keep warm.

2. While the pasta cooks, make the amatriciana sauce: Place a large, deep skillet over medium heat. Using kitchen shears, snip small, irregular pieces of bacon into the skillet. Cook, stirring, until bacon is crisp and fat is rendered, 4 to 5 minutes.

3. Coarsely chop the onions. Add the onions to the skillet, and cook, stirring, until softened, about 4 minutes. Stir in the tomatoes and the red pepper flakes, cover and bring to a boil over high heat. Reduce the heat to medium and simmer rapidly for 5 minutes.

step 2

prepare the **hearts of romaine salad with olives and marinated vegetables**

- 1 package (10 ounces) prewashed chopped romaine mix
- 2 tablespoons olive oil
- 1/2 cup jarred roasted red peppers with garlic, drained, some juices reserved, and sliced
- 1 cup giardiniera (Italian marinated vegetables salad), drained, some juices reserved
- 1/4 cup pitted kalamata olives

1. Toss the romaine with the olive oil and spread it over a large serving platter.

2. Drain and slice the roasted peppers, reserving some of the juices, and arrange them in a mound on the romaine. Drizzle a little of the pepper juice over the romaine.

3. Drain the giardiniera, again reserving a bit of the juice, and mound it on the romaine. Drizzle the romaine with some of the reserved juices.

4. Scatter the olives over the salad, grind some fresh black pepper over, and place the platter on the table.

step 3

serve

1. Stand the breadsticks in a glass.

2. Add the sauce to the pasta and toss. Divide among serving bowls and serve with the salad.

3. When ready for dessert, serve slices of the crumb cake with the chilled grapes.

Spaghetti Amatriciana
Single serving is 1/4 of total recipe
CALORIES 652; PROTEIN 19g; CARBS 106g; TOTAL FAT 14g; SAT FAT 3g; CHOLESTEROL 13mg; SODIUM 1424mg; FIBER 8g

pasta
with bacon, parmesan, and broccoli

green salad with olive vinaigrette

crusty bread

lemon raspberry sundaes

serves 4

shopping list

Pitted marinated olives

Prewashed spring greens mix

Shredded carrots
(from the salad bar
or produce department)

Lemon sorbet

Lemon nut cookies

Raspberry or strawberry
ice cream topping

Raspberries

Sliced bacon

Broccoli florets
(from the salad bar)

Vermicelli or other
thin-strand pasta

Parmesan cheese wedge

Crusty bread

from your pantry

Extra virgin olive oil

Rice vinegar

Salt

Freshly ground black pepper

Butter

beforeyoustart

Bring the water to a boil in a large pot, covered, over high heat to cook the pasta.

step	1	assemble the **green salad with olive vinaigrette**
step	2	assemble the **lemon raspberry sundaes**
step	3	cook the **pasta with bacon, parmesan, and broccoli**
step	4	**serve**

luckyforyou

For this one-pot pasta dish, we borrow the predominant flavorings from classic pasta à la carbonara—bacon, Parmesan cheese, and black pepper—but lighten things up a bit by omitting the cream and eggs that make it so rich. In their place we turn to a trick that Italians know well: reserving some pasta cooking water and tossing it with the hot pasta to achieve a properly moist consistency.

"One mouthful of this dish and you know it is the real deal. The pasta deserves genuine Parmigiano-Reggiano cheese."
—minutemeals' chef Sarah

step 1

assemble the **green salad with olive vinaigrette**

1/4 cup pitted marinated olives

1 tablespoon extra virgin olive oil

1 tablespoon rice vinegar

1 bag (5 ounces) prewashed spring greens mix

1/2 cup shredded carrots

1. Finely chop the olives. Combine the olives, oil, vinegar, and 1/4 teaspoon each salt and pepper in a serving bowl; stir to combine.

2. Add the salad mix and carrots to the dressing.

step 2

assemble the **lemon raspberry sundaes**

1 pint lemon sorbet

4 lemon nut cookies

1/2 cup raspberry or strawberry ice cream topping

1/2 pint fresh raspberries

1. Let the sorbet soften slightly before scooping into 4 dessert dishes. Place in the freezer.

2. Coarsely crumble the cookies.

step 3

cook the **pasta with bacon, parmesan, and broccoli**

8 slices bacon

4 cups broccoli florets

3/4 pound vermicelli or other thin strand pasta

2 tablespoons butter, cut into 4 pieces

3/4 cup freshly grated Parmesan cheese

1. Pour 4 quarts water into a large pot, salt lightly, and cover. Bring to a boil over high heat.

2. Meanwhile, cook the bacon in a microwave according to the package directions until crisp. Drain the bacon on paper towels. Cut the broccoli florets into bite-sized pieces.

3. Add the pasta to the boiling water and cook for 6 minutes. Add the broccoli and cook 2 minutes longer, until the pasta is *al dente* and the broccoli crisp-tender. While the pasta cooks, cut the bacon slices crosswise into 1/2-inch pieces. Cut the butter into 4 pieces. Grate enough Parmesan cheese to measure 3/4 cup.

4. Scoop out and reserve 1/2 cup of the pasta cooking water. Drain the pasta and broccoli in a colander. Return the pasta-cooking pot to the burner over the lowest possible heat. Add the butter, hot pasta, the reserved cooking water, the bacon, 1/2 cup Parmesan cheese, and 3/4 teaspoon freshly ground black pepper to the cooking pot. Toss the pasta well.

step 4

serve

1. Divide the pasta among 4 warm bowls. Pass the remaining 1/4 cup Parmesan cheese.

2. Toss the salad. Place the crusty bread on a cutting board with a serrated knife.

3. When ready for dessert, spoon raspberry sauce over the sorbet, and top each serving with some of the crumbled cookies and fresh raspberries.

Pasta with Bacon, Parmesan, and Broccoli
Single serving is 1/4 of total recipe
CALORIES 246; PROTEIN 27g; CARBS 15g;
TOTAL FAT 9g; SAT FAT 2g; CHOLESTEROL 63mg;
SODIUM 525mg; FIBER 3g

cauliflower and brown butter pasta
plum tomatoes with sweet onions and pepperoncini
lemon ice presto

menu
gameplan

serves 4

shopping list

Frozen lemonade concentrate

Cauliflower florets
(from the salad bar
or produce department)

Fresh refrigerated fettuccine

Fresh parsley

Plum tomatoes

Vidalia or other sweet
white onion

Jarred pepperoncini, cherry,
or banana pepper rings

from your pantry

Shaved ice

Salt and pepper

Butter

Seasoned dry bread crumbs
or coarsely chopped toasted
hazelnuts

Fruity olive oil

Red wine vinegar

beforeyoustart

Bring the water to a boil in a large
pot, covered, over high heat to cook
the fettuccine.

step **1** make the **lemon ice presto**

step **2** make the **cauliflower and brown butter pasta**

step **3** make the **tomatoes with onions and pepperoncini**

step **4** **serve**

headsup
If your refrigerator doesn't make crushed ice, ask the folks behind the seafood department counter at your supermarket to give you some. If they can't provide ice, place ice cubes in a self-sealing bag and crush with a rolling pin. Give the lemon ice a sophisticated zing by adding a tablespoon of chopped crystallized ginger.

"If you've ever tasted nutty, fragrant browned butter, you know that the whole stick used here is a justifiable indulgence."

—minutemeals' chef Wendy

step 1

make the **lemon ice presto**

3 cups shaved ice

1 can (12 ounces) frozen lemonade concentrate

1. Put the shaved ice and lemonade in a food processor. Pulse to mix.

2. Transfer the mixture to a metal bowl, cover with aluminum foil, and place in the freezer.

step 2

make the **cauliflower and brown butter pasta**

1 bag (12 ounces) cauliflower florets

1 pound fresh fettuccine

1/2 cup (1 stick) butter

1/3 cup seasoned dry bread crumbs or coarsely chopped toasted hazelnuts

1/3 cup chopped parsley

1. Pour 4 quarts water into a large pot, salt lightly, and cover. Bring to a boil over high heat.

2. Arrange the cauliflower florets in a single layer in a microwave-safe dish. Add 1/4 cup water, and cover with a lid or vented plastic wrap. Microwave on High for 6 to 8 minutes, until the cauliflower is crisp-tender.

3. Add the fettuccine to the water and cook for 2 to 3 minutes, until *al dente*. Drain.

4. In the pasta-cooking pot, melt the butter over medium heat. Continue to cook the butter for 2 minutes until it begins to foam and turn brown. Add the cauliflower and toss to coat. Add the fettuccine, bread crumbs or hazelnuts, and parsley and toss with 2 large spoons. Season with salt and pepper to taste.

step 3

make the **plum tomatoes with sweet onions and pepperoncini**

6 to 8 plum tomatoes

1/2 medium Vidalia or other sweet white onion

1/2 cup jarred pepperoncini, cherry, or banana pepper rings

2 tablespoons fruity olive oil

1 tablespoon red wine vinegar

1. Rinse the tomatoes and slice into thin wedges. Thinly slice the onion. Drain the pepper rings in a small strainer.

2. Arrange the plum tomatoes on a large platter. Spread the onion and peppers on top. Drizzle with the olive oil and vinegar, and season with salt and pepper to taste. Place the platter on the table with 4 salad plates.

step 4

serve

1. Divide the pasta among 4 serving bowls. Serve the pasta with the salad.

2. When ready for dessert, scoop the lemon ice into 4 dessert dishes and serve.

Cauliflower and Brown Butter Pasta
Single serving is 1/4 of total recipe

CALORIES 569; PROTEIN 15g; CARBS 74g; TOTAL FAT 26g; SAT FAT 15g; CHOLESTEROL 62mg; SODIUM 745mg; FIBER 6g

pasta
with red pepper vodka sauce

mixed green salad
with shaved parmesan

vanilla ice cream with espresso
sauce and mini chips

shopping list

Instant espresso powder

Spaghetti

Canned fire-roasted
tomatoes

Heavy cream

Prewashed baby greens
salad mix

Parmesan cheese wedge

Vanilla ice cream

Miniature chocolate chips

from your pantry

Light corn syrup

Salt

Vodka

Crushed red pepper flakes

Extra virgin olive oil

Red wine vinegar

Freshly ground black pepper

serves 4

beforeyoustart

Bring the water to a boil in a large
pot, covered, over high heat to cook
the spaghetti.

| step | 1 | make the **espresso sauce** |

| step | 2 | make the **pasta with red pepper vodka sauce** |

| step | 3 | make the **mixed green salad with shaved parmesan** |

| step | 4 | **serve** |

headsup

If you've never tasted
Parmigiano-Reggiano cheese,
you've missed one of the world's great cheeses. To make
sure you're getting the best, buy the cheese from a store
that moves products quickly, or, better yet, where you can
get a wedge freshly cut from a wheel. As the cut pieces
age, they dry out and the rich, nutty flavor becomes
merely sharp.

"Vodka imparts a subtle bite to the sauce—but you can omit it and still have wonderfully creamy, peppery pasta."

—minutemeals' chef Wendy

step 1

make the **espresso sauce**

¼ cup light corn syrup

1 tablespoon instant espresso powder

In a glass measuring cup, stir together the corn syrup and espresso powder. Set aside.

step 2

make the **pasta with red pepper vodka sauce**

1 pound spaghetti

2 cans (14 ounces each) fire-roasted tomatoes

2 cups heavy cream

¼ cup vodka

¾ to 1 teaspoon crushed red pepper flakes

1. Cook the pasta: Pour 4 quarts water into a large pot, salt lightly, and cover. Bring to a boil over high heat. Add the spaghetti and cook according to the directions on the package, until *al dente*. Drain in a colander.

2. While the pasta cooks, start the sauce: In a food processor, process the tomatoes, cream, vodka, and red pepper flakes.

3. After you drain the pasta, pour the tomato mixture into the empty pasta pot, cover and bring to a boil over low heat. Simmer 2 minutes, until slightly thickened. Season with salt to taste.

4. Add the pasta to the sauce and toss until well coated and hot.

step 3

make the **mixed green salad with shaved parmesan**

1 bag (5 ounces) prewashed baby greens salad mix

Parmesan cheese wedge

3 tablespoons extra virgin olive oil

1 tablespoon red wine vinegar

Place the greens in a salad bowl. With a vegetable peeler, shave a generous amount of Parmesan peelings onto the salad. Drizzle the olive oil and vinegar and grind some fresh black pepper over the salad, and toss gently. Place salad on the table with 4 salad plates.

step 4

serve

1. Bring the pasta to the table and divide it among 4 large pasta bowls. Serve with the salad.

2. When ready for dessert, scoop vanilla ice cream into 4 dessert dishes. Drizzle some espresso sauce over each serving, and sprinkle with miniature chocolate chips.

Pasta with Red Pepper Vodka Sauce
Single serving is ¼ of total recipe

CALORIES 865; PROTEIN 19g; CARBS 97g; TOTAL FAT 46g; SAT FAT 28g; CHOLESTEROL 163mg; SODIUM 811mg; FIBER 7g

pasta
with potatoes, green beans, and pesto
mozzarella and olives
breadsticks
chilled apricots with amaretti

shopping list

Macaroni or other small tubular pasta

Frozen cut green beans

Red-skinned potatoes

Pesto sauce

Fresh mozzarella or mild Gouda

Sweet or red onion slices (optional) (from the salad bar)

Green olives (jarred or from the salad bar)

Italian salad dressing

Breadsticks

Canned apricots packed in syrup (a 16-ounce can)

Amaretti

from your pantry

Salt

Shredded Parmesan cheese

serves 4

beforeyoustart

Bring the water to a boil in a large pot, covered, over high heat to cook the pasta. Chill the apricots.

| step | 1 | make the **pasta with potatoes, green beans, and pesto** |

| step | 2 | plate the **mozzarella and olives** |

| step | 3 | **serve** |

 Potatoes can take a while when cooked on the stove-top. For this recipe, we cook them in the microwave for all of 6 minutes.

"Pasta and potatoes are a classic in the north of Italy, and this delicious version only takes 20 minutes."

—minutemeals' chef Ruth

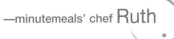

step 1

make the **pasta with potatoes, green beans, and pesto**

8 ounces macaroni or other small tubular pasta

1 package (8 to 9 ounces) frozen cut green beans

12 ounces small red-skinned potatoes

1/2 cup prepared pesto sauce

3/4 cup shredded Parmesan cheese

1. Pour 4 quarts water into a large pot, salt lightly, and cover. Bring the water to a boil over high heat. Add the macaroni, stir to separate, and cook according to the directions on the package until *al dente*. About 3 minutes before the pasta is finished, add the green beans to the pot and cook until just tender. Remove 1/2 cup of the pasta cooking water and reserve. Drain the pasta and beans well, return to the pot, and keep warm, covered.

2. While the pasta and beans are cooking, scrub the potatoes and cut them into 1/2-inch cubes. Place the cubes in a microwave-safe dish, add 1 tablespoon water, and cover. Microwave on High about 6 minutes, stirring once, until fork-tender.

step 2

plate the **mozzarella and olives**

Fresh mozzarella or mild Gouda

Sweet or red onion slices (optional)

Green and ripe olives of choice

2 tablespoons Italian salad dressing

1. Slice the mozzarella into as thin slices as possible and arrange around the outside rim of a platter.

2. Place the onion slices, if using, in the center of the platter, and scatter the olives over them. Drizzle the antipasto with the dressing and place the platter on the table with 4 salad plates.

step 3

serve

1. Transfer the pasta and green beans to a large serving bowl. Drain the potatoes and add to the bowl. Drop spoonfuls of the pesto over the pasta and vegetables and toss lightly, adding the reserved pasta cooking water if the mixture is too thick. Sprinkle with the shredded Parmesan cheese. Ladle the pasta at once into 4 large pasta bowls and serve.

2. Serve the mozzarella and olives as an accompaniment or as a starter with the breadsticks.

3. When ready for dessert, serve the apricots with some of their syrup in 4 dessert bowls with the amaretti as an accompaniment, or crumble them over the fruit.

Pasta with Potatoes, Green Beans, and Pesto
Single serving is 1/4 of total recipe
CALORIES 493; PROTEIN 18g; CARBS 65g;
TOTAL FAT 19g; SAT FAT 6g; CHOLESTEROL 19mg;
SODIUM 498mg; FIBER 3g

linguine
with caponata, ricotta, and basil

roasted asparagus

cucumbers and radishes

garlic breadsticks

hazelnut gelato and biscotti

menu
gameplan

shopping list

Asparagus

Fresh refrigerated linguine

Canned or jarred caponata eggplant appetizer

Fresh basil

Ricotta cheese

Cucumber slices
(from the salad bar)

Radishes
(from the salad bar)

Garlic breadsticks

Hazelnut gelato

Biscotti cookies

from your pantry

Extra virgin olive oil

Salt

Freshly ground black pepper

serves 4

beforeyoustart

Bring the water to a boil in a large pot, covered, over high heat to cook the pasta. Preheat the oven to 475°F to roast the asparagus.

step **1** prepare the **roasted asparagus**

step **2** cook the **linguine with caponata, ricotta, and basil**

step **3** serve

luckyforyou
Heating sauce in the pasta cooking pot means one less pot to wash. While the pasta drains, add the sauce to the pot and bring it to a boil over high heat. Then reduce the heat, and toss the pasta with the sauce for a minute or two—that's the Italian way. It helps each strand of pasta absorb some sauce and arrive at the table piping hot.

"When the fresh basil hits the hot pasta, the aroma will knock you out. That's what cooking is all about."

—minutemeals' chef David

step 1

prepare the **roasted asparagus**

1 pound asparagus, trimmed (keep the rubber band around the bunch and trim as directed below)

1 tablespoon extra virgin olive oil

1. Preheat the oven to 475°F. With the asparagus still bound by the rubber band, slice off about 1 inch of stalk from the end of the bunch. Remove the rubber band and place the asparagus in a shallow baking dish large enough to hold them in a single layer.

2. Drizzle the asparagus with the oil and sprinkle with ⅛ teaspoon salt. Toss to coat each stalk with oil; spread in a single layer. Roast until tender, 8 to 10 minutes.

step 2

cook the **linguine with caponata, ricotta, and basil**

12 ounces fresh linguine

2 cans (7½ ounces each) caponata eggplant appetizer

3 tablespoons extra virgin olive oil

½ cup fresh basil leaves

¾ cup ricotta cheese

1. Cook the pasta: Pour 4 quarts water into a large pot, salt lightly, and cover. Bring to a boil over high heat. Add the linguine and cook according to the directions on the package, until *al dente*. Drain in a colander.

2. Make the sauce: Return the empty pasta cooking pot to the stove over medium-high heat. Let the heat dry the pot for a few seconds. Add the caponata and olive oil and cook 2 minutes, stirring often, until hot. Add the linguine and toss well to coat. Cook 1 to 2 minutes, tossing frequently with 2 large spoons. Remove from the heat.

3. Stack the basil leaves and, using kitchen shears, snip thin strips of basil directly into the pasta. Toss and cover to keep warm.

step 3

serve

1. Transfer the asparagus to a platter. Place the cucumber slices and radishes on a plate. Stand the breadsticks in a glass. Bring all to the table with 4 salad plates.

2. Divide the linguine among 4 warm bowls and top each serving with about 3 tablespoons of ricotta cheese. Grind some fresh pepper over the cheese. Let diners toss their own linguine to distribute and melt the cheese.

3. When ready for dessert, place 2 scoops of gelato in each of 4 dessert bowls and top each with 2 cookies. Place on the table.

Linguine with Caponata, Ricotta, and Basil
Single serving is ¼ of total recipe

CALORIES 509; PROTEIN 14g; CARBS 56g; TOTAL FAT 25g; SAT FAT 7g; CHOLESTEROL 23mg; SODIUM 1551mg; FIBER 6g

macaroni
with broccoli rabe
antipasto
parmesan toasts
blueberries with orange sherbet

menu
gameplan

serves 4

beforeyoustart
Bring the water to a boil in a large pot, covered. Preheat the broiler.

shopping list

Macaroni

Broccoli rabe

Jarred marinated artichoke hearts

Jarred roasted red peppers

Jarred pepperoncini

Olives

Semolina bread

Blueberries, fresh or quick-thaw frozen

Orange sherbet

from your pantry

Salt

Garlic

Extra virgin olive oil

Dried red pepper flakes

Grated Parmesan cheese

step	1	make the **macaroni with broccoli rabe**
step	2	prepare the **antipasto**
step	3	make the **parmesan toasts**
step	4	prepare the **blueberries with orange sherbet**
step	5	**serve**

headsup Remember that the stems of broccoli rabe will take longer to cook than the leaves. It's a good idea, therefore, to add the stems to the skillet first, to allow them a little extra cooking time. Otherwise, they can be crisp to the point of being chewy.

"Eight cloves of garlic may seem like an enormous amount, but it's really not because it mellows when it cooks."

—minutemeals' chef Miriam

step 1

make the **macaroni with broccoli rabe**

1 box (16 ounces) macaroni

1 bunch broccoli rabe (about 1¼ pounds)

6 to 8 garlic cloves

⅓ cup extra virgin olive oil

¼ teaspoon dried red pepper flakes

1. Cook the pasta: Pour 4 quarts water into a large pot, salt lightly, and cover. Bring to a boil over high heat. Add the macaroni, stir to separate, and cook according to the directions on the package, stirring occasionally, until tender. Remove and reserve ½ cup of the pasta cooking liquid. Drain the macaroni well and return to the pot.

2. While the pasta cooks, make the sauce: Cut the tough stems off the broccoli rabe, then cut it into 1½-inch pieces. Slice the garlic.

3. In a large deep skillet, heat the olive oil over medium heat until warm. Add the garlic and red pepper flakes and cook, stirring occasionally, until the garlic is golden, about 3 minutes.

4. Add the broccoli rabe and cook over medium-high heat, stirring occasionally, about 3 or 4 minutes, until tender. Remove the pan from the heat and keep warm, covered.

step 2

prepare the **antipasto**

Jarred marinated artichoke hearts

Jarred roasted red peppers

Jarred pepperoncini

Olives

Drain each of the antipasto selections, then arrange on a large platter. Place the platter on the table with 4 salad plates.

step 3

make the **parmesan toasts**

1 loaf semolina bread

Extra virgin olive oil for brushing

Grated Parmesan cheese as needed

1. Preheat the broiler.

2. Cut the semolina loaf into ½-inch-thick slices. Brush the slices on both sides with extra virgin olive oil and place on a baking sheet. Broil about 4 inches from the heat until golden, about 1 minute. Turn and broil the second side until golden.

3. Sprinkle the rounds with Parmesan and broil for 1 minute, or until the cheese is melted. Place on a serving plate.

step 4

prepare the **blueberries with orange sherbet**

Fresh or thawed quick-thaw frozen blueberries

1 pint orange sherbet

1. If using fresh blueberries, pick them over and rinse in a colander. Let stand until serving time.

2. Remove the sherbet from the freezer to soften before serving.

step 5

serve

1. Add the broccoli rabe mixture and the reserved ½ cup pasta cooking liquid to the macaroni and toss well to combine. Season with salt, if desired. Cover and keep warm while having the antipasto platter with the Parmesan toasts.

2. Divide the macaroni and broccoli rabe among 4 pasta bowls or plates. Serve, with additional grated Parmesan, if desired.

3. When ready for dessert, scoop orange sherbet into 4 dessert bowls and scatter blueberries over the top. Serve, with the remaining blueberries, if desired.

Macaroni with Broccoli Rabe
Single serving is ¼ of total recipe
CALORIES 366; PROTEIN 10g; CARBS 41g;
TOTAL FAT 19g; SAT FAT 3g; CHOLESTEROL 0mg;
SODIUM 78mg; FIBER 3g

cheesy tortellini
with garlic
tomatoes balsamica
olive and rosemary bread
chocolate biscotti and long-stemmed strawberries

shopping list

Balsamic vinaigrette salad dressing

Prewashed mixed spring or baby greens

Tomatoes

Fresh refrigerated meat-filled tortellini

Fresh basil leaves

Ricotta cheese

Jarred roasted garlic in purée

Olive and rosemary bread

Chocolate biscotti

Long-stemmed strawberries

from your pantry

Dijon mustard

Salt

Freshly ground black pepper

Grated Parmesan cheese

serves 4

beforeyoustart

Bring the water to a boil in a large pot, covered, over high heat to cook the pasta. Rinse and chill the strawberries.

step **1** make the **tomatoes balsamica**

step **2** cook the **cheesy tortellini with garlic**

step **3** serve

 **lucky**foryou Slightly sweet, mellow, and buttery, roasted garlic is now sold in jars at the supermarket. You can use it in place of (or in addition to) fresh garlic in most recipes; it's especially useful in dishes that don't get cooked, where it contributes wonderful flavor without raw-garlic bite. You can even spread it on bread—it's that mild, and without the fat and calories found in butter.

"I use ricotta cheese for its creamy texture, and Parmesan for its bite—a winning combination, and easier than cream sauce."

—minutemeals' chef Paul

step 1
make the **tomatoes balsamica**

1/4 cup bottled balsamic vinaigrette salad dressing

1 1/2 tablespoons Dijon mustard

1 package (5 ounces) prewashed spring or baby greens

4 ripe medium tomatoes

1. Whisk together the vinaigrette and mustard in a small bowl. Arrange the salad mix on 4 salad plates.

2. Slice the tomatoes and arrange on top of the greens. Season with salt and a good grinding of freshly ground pepper to taste. Place the salads and dressing on the table.

step 2
cook the **cheesy tortellini with garlic**

1 pound fresh meat-filled tortellini

1/3 cup fresh basil leaves

1 1/4 cups ricotta cheese

2/3 cup grated Parmesan cheese

1 tablespoon jarred roasted garlic in purée

1. Cook the pasta: Pour 4 quarts water into a large pot, salt lightly, and cover. Bring to a boil over high heat. Add the tortellini and cook, stirring often, for 8 to 10 minutes, or until just tender. Scoop out and reserve 1 cup of the cooking water and drain the tortellini in a colander.

2. Stack and thinly slice the basil leaves. Return the reserved cup of water to the pasta pot. Stir in the ricotta, Parmesan, garlic, and pepper. Bring to a simmer over medium heat and cook 2 minutes, whisking occasionally. Remove from the heat and gently stir in the tortellini.

step 3
serve

1. Slice the bread and place in a napkin-lined basket.

2. Add the sliced basil to the tortellini and divide among 4 serving bowls.

3. Let diners drizzle some of the dressing over their salads.

4. When ready for dessert, serve the biscotti and strawberries.

Cheesy Tortellini with Garlic
Single serving is 1/4 of total recipe
CALORIES 439; PROTEIN 30g; CARBS 24g;
TOTAL FAT 24g; SAT FAT 13g; CHOLESTEROL 196mg;
SODIUM 789g; FIBER 1g

salsa pasta olé

green salad with chili vinaigrette

honeyed cantaloupe with blueberries

menu gameplan

serves 4

beforeyoustart

Bring a large pot of water, covered, to a boil over high heat to cook the pasta. Preheat the broiler.

step 1 — make the **salsa pasta olé**

step 2 — assemble the **green salad with chili vinaigrette**

step 3 — prepare the **honeyed cantaloupe with blueberries**

step 4 — **serve**

---

shopping list

Fresh refrigerated cheese tortelloni

Fully cooked chicken or turkey sausage

Mild chunky salsa

Pre-shredded Monterey Jack cheese

Prewashed baby salad greens with fresh herbs

Raw or toasted pumpkin seeds, shelled

Lemon (for juice)

Blueberries

Cantaloupe cubes (from the produce department)

from your pantry

Salt

Grated Parmesan cheese

Vinaigrette salad dressing

Chili powder

Ground cumin

Honey

Ground cinnamon

luckyforyou Fresh pasta, even filled fresh pasta, cooks quickly.

"What to do with fresh cheese tortelloni besides tossing it with marinara sauce? How about a Mexican casserole?" —minutemeals' chef Sarah

step 1

make the **salsa pasta olé**

2 packages (9 ounces each) fresh cheese tortelloni

¹/₂ pound fully cooked chicken or turkey sausage

1 jar (16 ounces) mild chunky salsa

1 cup pre-shredded Monterey Jack cheese

¹/₄ cup grated Parmesan cheese

1. Cook the pasta: Pour 4 quarts water into a large pot, salt lightly, and cover. Bring to a boil over high heat. Add the tortelloni, stir to separate, and cook according to the directions on the package. Drain in a colander.

2. While the pasta cooks, start the sauce: Preheat the broiler.

3. Slice the sausage. In a medium nonstick skillet, cook the sausage over medium-high heat, stirring frequently, until it begins to brown lightly, about 3 minutes. Remove the skillet from the heat.

4. In the same pot used to cook the pasta, bring the salsa to a boil. Remove the pot from the heat; stir in the tortelloni, ¹/₂ cup of the Monterey Jack cheese, and the sausage until well combined.

5. Spoon the pasta into a metal broiler-proof 2¹/₂-quart casserole. Top with the remaining ¹/₂ cup Monterey Jack cheese and the Parmesan. Broil 5 to 6 inches from the heat for 2 to 3 minutes, until browned on the top and bubbly.

step 2

assemble the **green salad with chili vinaigrette**

2 tablespoons vinaigrette salad dressing

¹/₄ teaspoon chili powder

¹/₄ teaspoon ground cumin

1 bag (5 ounces) prewashed baby salad greens with fresh herbs

2 tablespoons raw or toasted shelled pumpkin seeds

In a large bowl, stir together the vinaigrette, chili powder, and cumin until blended. Add the salad greens and pumpkin seeds. Place the bowl on the table.

step 3

prepare the **honeyed cantaloupe with blueberries**

1 tablespoon fresh lemon juice (1 lemon)

2 tablespoons honey

Pinch of ground cinnamon

1 cup fresh blueberries

3 cups cantaloupe cubes

1. Squeeze lemon juice into a medium bowl. Add the honey and cinnamon and whisk until blended.

2. Pick over the blueberries, rinse, and drain well.

3. Add the blueberries and cantaloupe to the lemon honey and toss gently to coat.

step 4

serve

1. Place the pasta casserole on the table. Spoon the pasta into 4 pasta bowls and serve.

2. Toss the salad at the table and serve.

3. When ready for dessert, spoon the fruit and honey syrup into 4 dessert dishes. Serve.

Salsa Pasta Olé
Single serving is ¹/₄ of total recipe
CALORIES 629; PROTEIN 37g; CARBS 66g;
TOTAL FAT 23g; SAT FAT 14g; CHOLESTEROL 94mg;
SODIUM 1905mg; FIBER 4g

tofu fried rice

gingered chicken soup with spinach

sesame snow peas with carrots

rainbow sherbet with cream wafers

menu gameplan

serves 4

shopping list

Firm tofu

Frozen mixed vegetables

Stir-fry sauce

Gingerroot

Lemon- and garlic-flavored chicken broth

Prewashed baby spinach

Sliced scallions (from the salad bar)

Snow peas (pretrimmed, if possible, from the produce department)

Matchstick-cut carrots (from the produce department)

Rainbow sherbet

Cream wafers

from your pantry

Toasted sesame oil

Leftover cooked rice

Peanut oil

Sesame seeds

Lite soy sauce

beforeyoustart

Defrost the frozen vegetables in the microwave according to the directions on the package.

step 1 stir-fry the **tofu fried rice**

step 2 make the **gingered chicken soup with spinach**

step 3 cook the **sesame snow peas with carrots**

step 4 serve

headsup Fried rice should be made with cold rice; if the rice is hot, the grains will stick together when fried. That takes some planning—you'll need to either make a batch of rice or pick up or order takeout ahead of time. If you don't have leftovers but do have extra time, cook a fresh batch of Minute Rice, spread it on a baking sheet, and freeze it for 30 minutes before frying.

"Fried rice is a vehicle for leftovers. In China, it's traditional to add what's on hand, so it's different every time."

—minutemeals' chef David

step 1

stir-fry the **tofu fried rice**

12 ounces firm tofu,
drained and patted dry

1 cup frozen mixed vegetables,
thawed

4 teaspoons toasted
sesame oil

4 cups cooked rice

1/2 cup prepared stir-fry sauce

1. Cut tofu into 1/4-inch cubes. Thaw the vegetables in the microwave according to package directions.

2. Heat 2 teaspoons of the oil in a large nonstick skillet over medium-high heat. Add the tofu and stir-fry 3 to 4 minutes until lightly browned. Add the vegetables and stir-fry 2 minutes longer. Transfer to a bowl.

3. Add the remaining 2 teaspoons oil to the skillet. Add the rice and cook, stirring often, for 3 to 4 minutes or until heated through. Add the cooked tofu, the vegetables, and the stir-fry sauce and stir-fry 2 minutes longer, until heated through. Remove from the heat and cover to keep warm.

step 2

make the **gingered chicken soup with spinach**

2-inch knob fresh gingerroot,
unpeeled, thinly sliced

2 cans (14 1/2 ounces each)
lemon- and garlic-flavored
chicken broth

1 bag (5 ounces) prewashed
baby spinach

1/4 cup sliced scallions

1. Thinly slice the gingerroot. Place it in a heavy medium saucepan with the chicken broth, cover, and bring to a boil over medium-high heat. Reduce the heat and simmer for 2 minutes.

2. Remove the soup from the heat. Stir in the spinach and cover to keep warm.

step 3

cook the **sesame snow peas with carrots**

1/2-inch piece peeled fresh
gingerroot

12 ounces snow peas,
pretrimmed if available

1 tablespoon peanut oil

1 cup matchstick-cut carrots

1 tablespoon lite soy sauce

1. Finely chop the ginger. Trim the ends of the snow peas if necessary.

2. Heat the oil in a large nonstick skillet over medium-high heat. Add the ginger and cook, stirring, 30 seconds, until fragrant. Add the snow peas and the carrots and stir-fry 3 to 4 minutes, until the snow peas are bright green and crisp-tender. Add the soy sauce and stir-fry 30 seconds longer.

step 4

serve

1. Remove the sliced ginger from the soup. Ladle soup into 4 small bowls and sprinkle 1 tablespoon of scallions over each serving.

2. Divide the tofu fried rice and the snow peas and carrots among 4 dinner plates and serve.

3. When ready for dessert, scoop the rainbow sherbet into 4 dessert dishes. Stand 2 cream wafers in each dish and serve.

Tofu Fried Rice
Single serving is 1/4 of total recipe
CALORIES 373; PROTEIN 16g; CARBS 57g;
TOTAL FAT 9g; SAT FAT 1g; CHOLESTEROL 0mg;
SODIUM 1088mg; FIBER 2g

paella
mixed green salad with olives
flan with figs

---

shopping list

Spanish rice and sauce mix

Precooked andouille, chorizo, or other spicy sausage

Medium shrimp, peeled and deveined

Flat-leaf parsley

Prewashed mixed baby greens

Pitted olives

Italian salad dressing

Fresh or dried figs

Flan

from your pantry

Extra virgin olive oil

Salt and pepper

serves 4

step **1** make the **paella**

step **2** assemble the **mixed green salad with olives**

step **3** **serve**

luckyforyou Using precooked sausage is one of the things that makes this dish doable in 20 minutes. (Already peeled and deveined shrimp is another.) Classic Spanish paella is traditionally made with chorizo, a sausage made with either fresh or smoked pork, garlic, chili powder, and other seasoning. We used andouille sausage, the spicy, smoky pork sausage that is a staple of Cajun cooking.

"Appearances count, and here's a secret for making less look like more: Time permitting, halve the shrimp lengthwise."

—minutemeals' chef Wendy

step 1

make the **paella**

1 bag (5.6 ounces) Spanish rice and sauce mix

2 tablespoons extra virgin olive oil

8 ounces precooked andouille, chorizo, or other spicy sausage

8 ounces peeled and deveined medium shrimp, rinsed and patted dry

1/3 cup chopped fresh flat-leaf parsley

1. Cook the rice mix according to the directions on the package, using 1 tablespoon olive oil instead of butter. Slice the sausage on the diagonal 1/4 inch thick. Rinse the shrimp and pat dry. Chop enough parsley to measure 1/3 cup.

2. In a large skillet, heat the remaining 1 tablespoon of olive oil over moderately high heat. Cook the sausage until heated through and browned. Add the shrimp and cook about 4 minutes longer, tossing frequently, until pink and firm.

3. Add the cooked rice to the skillet and toss to evenly distribute the sausage and shrimp. Add the chopped parsley and toss to combine. Cover to keep warm.

step 2

assemble the **mixed green salad with olives**

1 bag (5 ounces) prewashed mixed baby greens

1/2 cup pitted olives

1/4 cup Italian salad dressing

In a salad bowl combine the greens and olives. Toss gently with the salad dressing and salt and pepper to taste. Place the salad on the table.

step 3

serve

1. Fluff the paella with a fork and bring it to the table. Serve the paella with the salad.

2. When ready for dessert, rinse the fresh figs, if using. Place the fresh or dried figs in a bowl and serve with the flan.

Paella
Single serving is 1/4 of total recipe
CALORIES 495; PROTEIN 25g; CARBS 32g;
TOTAL FAT 29g; SAT FAT 9g; CHOLESTEROL 131mg;
SODIUM 1355mg; FIBER 1g

moroccan couscous and vegetables

spinach salad with mandarin oranges

dates, apricots, and almond macaroons

shopping list

Frozen mixed carrots, cauliflower, and broccoli

Chickpeas

Couscous

Canned mandarin oranges

Prewashed baby spinach

Poppyseed salad dressing

Ripe fresh apricots
(or juice-packed canned)

Dates

Almond macaroons

from your pantry

Olive oil

Ground cumin

Salt and pepper

menu gameplan

serves 4

beforeyoustart

Bring the water to a boil in a medium saucepan, covered. Chill the canned or rinse and chill the fresh apricots.

step 1 — cook the **moroccan couscous and vegetables**

step 2 — make the **spinach salad with mandarin oranges**

step 3 — **serve**

headsup

Heating the ground cumin in oil mellows the spice so that it enriches the finished dish instead of overwhelming it. Take a minute or so to warm ground or whole dried spices whenever you use them, whether they will be cooked further with additional ingredients or stirred into a cold dish.

"I developed the couscous to capture the flavors of the Mediterranean in my home, in a hurry."

—minutemeals' chef Ruth

step 1
cook the **moroccan couscous and vegetables**

- 3 tablespoons olive oil
- 2 teaspoons ground cumin
- 1 bag (16 ounces) frozen mixed carrots, cauliflower, and broccoli
- 1 can (15 to 16 ounces) chickpeas, drained and rinsed
- 1 package (10 ounces) couscous

1. Place 2 tablespoons olive oil and the cumin in a large nonstick skillet over medium heat. Cook, stirring constantly, 1 to 2 minutes, or until aromatic.

2. Add the frozen vegetables and toss to coat with the oil. Stir-fry for 3 minutes. Drain and rinse the chickpeas and add them to the skillet. Add 1 cup water and bring to a boil. Cover, reduce the heat to medium-low, and cook until the vegetables are tender, about 8 minutes. Season with salt and pepper to taste.

3. Meanwhile, in a medium saucepan, prepare the couscous as directed on the package, adding the remaining 1 tablespoon olive oil. Cover and let stand while vegetables finish cooking.

step 2
make the **spinach salad with mandarin oranges**

- 1 can (6 ounces) mandarin oranges, drained
- 1 bag (5 ounces) prewashed baby spinach
- 3 to 4 tablespoons poppyseed salad dressing

1. Drain the oranges.

2. Place the spinach in a salad bowl, top with the oranges, and add the dressing. Toss to coat. Place the salad on the table.

step 3
serve

1. Season the couscous with salt and pepper and fluff with a fork. Divide the couscous among 4 dinner plates, making mounds with a large well in the center of each. Spoon the vegetable mixture into the wells, and spoon the pan juices over the top. Serve with the salad.

2. When ready for dessert, place the canned apricots, if using, in 4 dessert dishes, or place the fresh apricots on a plate or in a bowl filled with ice cubes. Arrange the dates and almond macaroons on a dessert plate and serve with the apricots.

Moroccan Couscous and Vegetables
Single serving is ¼ of total recipe

CALORIES 461; PROTEIN 15g; CARBS 73g; TOTAL FAT 12g; SAT FAT 2g; CHOLESTEROL 0mg; SODIUM 411mg; FIBER 10g

cheddary micro-baked potatoes

spinach salad with egg

frozen chocolate yogurt and orange cookies

serves 4

shopping list

Baking potatoes

Pre-shredded extra-sharp Cheddar, Monterey Jack, or Swiss cheese

Reduced-fat sour cream

Oil-packed sun-dried tomatoes

Prewashed baby spinach leaves

Red wine vinegar vinaigrette dressing

Frozen chocolate yogurt

Orange cookies

from the salad bar

Chopped scallions

Cherry or grape tomatoes

Peeled hard-cooked eggs

from your pantry

Salt

Freshly ground black pepper

menu gameplan

step **1** make the **cheddary micro-baked potatoes**

step **2** assemble the **spinach salad with egg**

step **3** serve

luckyforyou There's time in this menu to grate a piece of Cheddar if that's all you have in the fridge.

"Even after the most exhausting day, you can get it together to make this! And you'll be glad you did."

—minutemeals' chef Hillary

step 1

make the **cheddary micro-baked potatoes**

4 medium (8 ounces each) baking potatoes

1 1/2 cups pre-shredded extra-sharp Cheddar, Monterey Jack, or Swiss cheese

1/2 cup reduced-fat sour cream

1/4 cup chopped scallions

1. Pierce the potatoes in several places with a fork. Place 1 potato in the center of the microwave tray and the other 3 around it like spokes on a wheel. Microwave on High for 14 to 16 minutes, or until tender. Carefully slit each potato and allow to cool 1 minute.

2. While the potatoes bake, in a medium bowl, stir together well the Cheddar, sour cream, scallions, 1/4 teaspoon salt, and 1/8 teaspoon pepper.

step 2

assemble the **spinach salad with egg**

2 tablespoons chopped oil-packed sun-dried tomatoes

1/2 cup cherry or grape tomatoes

1 bag (5 ounces) prewashed baby spinach leaves

3 tablespoons red wine vinegar vinaigrette dressing

2 peeled hard-cooked eggs

1. Chop enough sun-dried tomatoes, drained, to measure 2 tablespoons.

2. Rinse the cherry or grape tomatoes and pat dry.

3. Place the spinach, cherry or grape tomatoes, and sun-dried tomatoes in a large salad bowl. Add the vinaigrette and toss.

4. Quarter the eggs and place the wedges on the salad. Place the bowl on the table.

step 3

serve

1. Place each potato on a dinner plate. With the back of a fork, mash the insides of each. Top the halves with the Cheddar mixture, dividing it evenly among the potatoes, and stir it in to combine. Serve the potatoes with the salad.

2. When ready for dessert, scoop the frozen yogurt into 4 dessert bowls and serve it with the cookies.

Cheddary Micro-Baked Potatoes
Single serving is 1/4 of total recipe

CALORIES 358; PROTEIN 16g; CARBS 38g; TOTAL FAT 16g; SAT FAT 10g; CHOLESTEROL 49mg; SODIUM 454mg; FIBER 3g

d

e

f

W

Wafers, store-bought

    chocolate, **140–41**

    chocolate cream, raspberry-banana compote and, **126–27**

    cream, rainbow sherbet with, **162–63**

Walnut

    Jarlsberg cheese and, salad, **6–7**

    Parmesan-, pitas, **20–21**

Warm Chocolate Chip and Caramel Cookies, **60–61**

Watercress

    beet, and apple salad, **66–67**

    and Red Onion Salad, **16–17**

    Rice, **112–13**

Watermelon, store-bought

    Chunks with Amaretti Cookies, **142–43**

    lime-marinated, with blackberries, **42–43**

Wheat

    cracked, Italian bread, with dipping oil, **24–25**

    whole-, pita bread, **12–13**

Whole-Grain Italian Bread, **140–41**

Whole-Grain Rolls, **40–41**

Winter squash, maple-and-spice, **40–41**

Y

Yellow rice. *See* Rice

Yogurt, store-bought

    frozen chocolate, and orange cookies, **168–69**

    frozen, with bananas and caramel sauce, **40–41**

    with Honey, Apricots, and Pistachios, **100–101**

    spinach with, **72–73**

Z

Zucchini, stewed tomatoes and, **118–19**